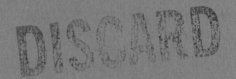

Retire to Action

A Guide to Voluntary Service

Retire to Action

A Guide to Voluntary Service

Julietta K. Arthur

Introduction by
Senator Harrison A. Williams, Jr.

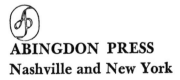

ABINGDON PRESS
Nashville and New York

RETIRE TO ACTION: A GUIDE TO VOLUNTARY SERVICE

Copyright © 1969 by The Estate of Julietta K. Arthur

Standard Book Number: 687-36218-0
Library of Congress Catalog Card Number: 70-86160

SET UP, PRINTED, AND BOUND BY
THE PARTHENON PRESS, AT NASHVILLE,
TENNESSEE, UNITED STATES OF AMERICA

To the memory of Louis
who led a meaningful life

"Equating work with well-being, we are sometimes told is an outmoded concept. . . . Those who will retire in the 1960's, however, are generally unprepared for inactivity. They are work-oriented. . . . [Those] who started their careers in the depression years of the '30's, often carried great responsibilities in the War Years of the '40's, and confronted the challenges of the rapidly changing world of the '50's . . . had neither the time nor the inclination for leisure. Our whole society, furthermore, is work-oriented.

"Patterns of a career lifetime are seldom altered abruptly. Most [people] in retirement will continue to feel the need for useful and meaningful activity."

New Directions
Published for prospective retirees from
Foreign Affairs Agencies by the State Department
August, 1966

Introduction

"I have had quite a little success, but I am still hoping for more, and the two children I am working with are cooperating with me. As for my own health, I think it has been the best thing for me that there is, because now I don't sit around the house reading newspapers or anything else like that. . . . I still owe something to it [her home community], and if it is only just to go up and help those mentally retarded children in Willowbrook, I feel as though I am doing something. It gives me an uplift."

> From testimony by a sixty-four-year-old volunteer in Project SERVE, at a hearing on a proposed "Nationwide Older American Community Service Program," September 19, 1967, Washington, D.C.

Americans have always thought of this nation as a land of plenty, but even the most abundant resources can become exhausted or tragically marred by exploitation or just plain carelessness. Our population is plagued by fouled streams, dirty air, the loss of forests and fields to senseless urban sprawl, and other assaults upon an environment called upon to support growing numbers of people.

Our waste of human skills and energies is even more appalling. As long as there is a youngster whose future is blighted by deprivation or hopelessness, we deny ourselves full access to all the talents we need to keep this nation great. As long as there is an American of any age disabled by preventable disease or accident, we are wasting manpower and permitting pain to take a needless toll.

And, if we permit ourselves to remain blind to the potential services that retired Americans can render to their fellow Americans, we shall be guilty of new and equally unforgiveable waste.

Ten or twenty years ago, we could not talk with such urgency about the need for service roles in retirement.

But now, we not only can; we must.

Persons at or past age sixty-five now number about twenty million in the United States. And there are about an equal number in their late fifties or early sixties. In other words, about one-fifth of our population is now concerned—or should be concerned—about making the best possible use of the retirement to which they are entitled after decades in the national labor force.

There is no doubt that millions of older Americans have earned a right to a period of leisure and thought. It is also true that many Americans of advanced years are cruelly hampered by chronic illness. For them, the opportunity to give service may be neither attractive nor possible.

For many Americans—perhaps millions of others—retirement could well be the time in life best suited for giving service.

Julietta Arthur, the author of the informative chapters that follow, has recognized that this nation is now in the early stages of a "retirement revolution" that could lead to a "service revolution" among our elders. The retirement revolution is taking shape because more Americans are spending more years in retirement. As life expectancy increases, the average work life decreases. Some Americans now retire in their late fifties or early sixties, rather than at sixty-five; and there is a strong possibility that accelerating gains in productivity could result in even earlier retirement or alternative adjustments in customary work life patterns.

Whatever form it takes, "free time" is certain to become a greater force in American life than it now is. Why should we believe that an increase in "free time" will result in an intensified desire to give service?

One answer to that question is already provided in the pilot programs in operation through the auspices of the Office of Economic Opportunity, the Department of Labor, and the U.S. Administration on Aging. The programs, described so well by Mrs. Arthur, give older Americans an opportunity to work in neighborhoods and in institutions where the need for service is great. Many elderly participants are frank to say that they depend heavily upon the modest compensation provided in some projects—they could not otherwise make ends meet without such earnings. Others are unpaid volunteers, such as the woman quoted at the beginning of this chapter.

Whether paid or not, practically every older participant to whom I have spoken privately or at hearings tells of the deep satisfaction derived from performing worthwhile work that would probably not have been done if he had not made himself available to do it. And, if you do not happen to realize at this point that the backlog of service needs is great and growing, I refer you to the hundreds of examples of needs provided by Mrs. Arthur in this book.

Among the many other merits of Mrs. Arthur's volume is that she gives Americans full credit for being as individualistic after retirement as they were before. Tastes and talents vary when selecting a retirement service role as in making other major decisions throughout life. To provide the widest possible choice, the author provides an impressive catalogue of service opportunities now available through private and public agencies.

Mrs. Arthur is too down-to-earth to think of herself as a prophet, but she has provided the reader with powerful evidence of the shape of things to come in terms of meaningful retirement through service to others. There is every reason to agree with former Secretary of Labor Wirtz, who said before a Congressional Subcommittee:

I expect that before we are through with this we are going to find a whole new concept of what people do after age 60 or 65. I don't think we are looking 50 years ahead. I think we are looking 5 or 10 years ahead. I see the emergence, with the development of technology and the affluent society . . . I see the emergence of a whole new concept of what people do, are supposed to do, and how they are paid for it, how they are compensated for it after they finish what we presently call employment.[1]

---

[1] Secretary Wirtz was testifying at a hearing on a bill introduced by Senator Williams, who called for establishment of an "Older Americans' Community Service Program" that would provide incentives for private and public agencies to meet service needs in the home communities by paid or volunteer elderly participants. At the time of this writing, Senator Williams was revising his bill to incorporate suggestions made as a result of the hearings and other developments.

Undoubtedly, government can help stimulate the climate in which new service opportunities can be developed—as well as other changes implied in Mr. Wirtz's statement—but a more fundamental force will be a change of attitude in what Americans expect out of retirement. The end of work should not be regarded as the beginning of a bleak wait for death. Retirement *can be* a satisfying period of challenge and development, made richer in many ways for those willing and able to provide service to others.

Harrison A. Williams, Jr. (N.J.)
Chairman, Special Committee on Aging,
United States Senate

In Acknowledgment

This is the kind of book which could never have been written without candid revelations of many men and women, both those already retired from business or the professions and those looking ahead to retirement. In both groups there were many jubilant at the thought of the increased opportunities more leisure would give them, and those who were apprehensive. All of them, through letters or interviews, cooperated freely in talking frankly about their experiences and their plans (or lack of them). Some had succeeded in overcoming the inertia of society and its general unpreparedness to use the talents of those who have lived long enough to want to work in a concerned way. In a few cases I have been able to relate their stories so that others could benefit. The majority must remain unknown to readers of this book simply because there were too many generous enough to relate their experiences, to mention them in this limited space. I would like to thank all those who answered my letters or talked to me, for their honesty and for the many helpful suggestions they made so that others would not have to suffer from enforced inactivity.

The second large group to whom I owe much is the large number of dedicated staff members of Federal and State organizations who have taken time out of busy days and crowded schedules to give me information, to help me verify or track down elusive facts, and to answer what must often have seemed numerous queries on technical matters. That there is increasing awareness of the potentialities of older people, and their value for the country at large, is indicated not only by the increased flow of legislation on their behalf, but the very real interest taken in this book by staff members whose own retirement years are many years ahead. It is impossible because of lack of space to name them individually, but I would like to express my gratitude to them and to the executives of the following divisions of our Federal government: the Staff of the Administration on Aging, Social and Rehabilitation Service of the U.S. Department of Health, Education, and Welfare, and all the heads of its Regional offices; the U.S. Department of Agriculture and many of its Extension Service agents; the U.S. Department of Commerce; the National Institute of Mental Health, U.S. Public Health Service; the U.S. Department of Labor, and in particular, its Employment Service, its Office of Special Manpower Programs, and its Service to Older Workers; the Small Business Administration; and finally, the State Department.

It would be ungracious not to acknowledge the vast amount of help and information I have received from many state organizations, members of the National Association of State Units on Aging. Many of them have pioneered in developing projects to which older Americans are contributing their skills and interest.

Far too many organizations in the nonprofit field, from coast to coast, have given me the benefit of rich experiences in making use of older people's participation to further their work to enable me to acknowledge their aid. I can only mention specifically many multi-purpose centers and volunteer service bureaus, in large communities and small ones, which have made available accumulated data showing a resourceful use of older people's capacities and capabilities in many different areas.

Finally, there is a group of informed men and women who have helped me avoid errors of fact, interpretation, and judgment, by reading critically, sometimes in more than one version, chapters that dealt with their special interests and knowledge of my subject. I have leaned heavily on the wisdom of Gerald A. Bloedow, Executive Secretary, Governor's Citizens Council on Aging of the state of Minnesota; Mrs. Janet W. Freund, Coordinator, Project for Academic Motivation, Public Schools, Winnetka, Illinois; David Jeffreys, Director, National Affairs, American Association of Retired Persons and National Retired Teachers Association; Mrs. Eone Harger, Director, New Jersey Division on Aging, Department of Community Affairs; Eleanor Morris, Associate Commissioner, Region II, Administration on Aging, and Mrs. Maxine Keir of her New York staff; Mrs. Anne B. Nicholson, Director, Volunteer Service Bureau, Minneapolis; William E. Oriol, Staff Director, U.S. Senate Special Committee on Aging; James H. Parke, Director, Volunteer Service Staff, Veterans Administration; Marie Ponzo, Libarian, and Mrs. Alice Wolfson, Assistant to the Director, National Council on the Aging; Edward V. Pope, Human Development and Human Relations Specialist, U.S. Department of Agriculture; Edwin H. Powers, Assistant Director, Office of Public Relations, American National Red Cross; Mrs. Virginia Smyth, Regional Commissioner, Social and Rehabilitation Service, U.S. Department of Health, Education and Welfare, Atlanta, Ga.

To all of them go my thanks for their aid and for their interest.

Julietta K. Arthur

Contents

Chapter I

Achieving
Retirement Goals

In our time there is nothing extraordinary in living ten, twenty, or even thirty years past a sixty-fifth birthday and being in full possession of one's faculties. With this prospect before you, you ought not to drift and run the risk of boredom—or worse—as the years roll on. If you are still at the stage when you can look ahead before one door shuts behind you, stride boldly forward and investigate what lies behind the retirement portal in front of you. If you are already on its threshold you still have time to make a choice between the routes Dr. William H. Reals pointed out. In a booklet he dedicated to a group of St. Louis business and professional men who decided to pool their talents to serve their community, he said this: "One has more time after retirement to rock, more time to fish, more time to loaf and rust out, or more time to do the challenging things one has always wanted to do but couldn't because of the alarm clock and time schedule."

The idea that people in their later years should and can be deeply interested in finding "some place where they can invest their humanity," as Dr. Albert Schweitzer put it, would have seemed ludicrous only a few years ago. But all over the country this is what is happening. Men and women who realize they will probably live approximately twenty years longer than their fathers did at the turn of this century are not content to accept the dictionary's definition of retirement as "withdrawal" or "retreat." They know it is an outmoded concept. They are also the ones who are not waiting for someone else to point out that the greatest need in America today is for a few million citizens to become involved in society's problems.

Scientists predict that by the year 2000 the life-span may well be around a hundred years. What is more important in the here and now is that you have an excellent chance of being hale and hearty at an age at which your immediate ancestors counted themselves fortunate if they could still hug the hearthside. The very fact that society has not yet worked out all the roles older men and women can play is in itself a tremendous challenge. For no other generation in its fifties, sixties, or even in its seventh or eighth decades, has had the chance to forge its own pattern of living to the extent this one has.

Retirement Goals

A successful retirement goal, however, has to be centered around something more than "a place to live, something to do, and someone to care." It requires reasonably good health, both physical and emotional, if possible, or adjustment—not resignation—to disability when or if it comes, plus a determination to remain mentally active. Nor can one stop even at acquiring these desirables.

Those who count on spending their remaining days just in "enjoying life" or achieving a more adequate income, or attempt to wrap their lives around their children or their grandchildren, will have considerable success in encountering frustration. No one can expect happiness in retirement as a right to which he is entitled; nearly always it has to be earned, sometimes painfully. On the other hand, life need not be regarded as a book in which retirement is the last chapter. The later years are part of a continuity of experiences from babyhood on, not a sharp break after middle-age. All the experiences of life, good and bad, and the wisdom that ought to be acquired through them, is what everyone should count on to see him safely to the end. But he must learn how to make good use of them.

22

All the successfully retired people—the septuagenarians or the octogenarians about whom someone is always exclaiming, "Isn't he (or she) amazing?" or "How do they do it at their age?" have found an interest in life, and in particular, in other human beings' fates. This type of person is always able to make a good adjustment to whatever comes, be it joy or sorrow.

The Time to Plan

Nobody among the experts has come up with a cut and dried date when planning for retirement should start. But in this era, when one can easily spend perhaps a third of his life away from a paid job or a profession he has worked hard and long at, the consensus is that the earlier anybody starts to think of his future years, the better they are likely to be. A corollary to that statement is that it is never too late to begin. (A Methodist church in Oklahoma City has developed the School of Continuing Education for Senior Adults. The program is said to have received its initial impetus from an eighty-three-year-old woman who had observed her peers slipping into senility and concluded that "the health of the brain and its capacity to function seem to depend on the mental exercise of the learning process.")

Anybody who has a chance to participate in pre-retirement courses or individual counseling, which some industries and government circles offer, ought to take advantage of them, if only to have a focus for his own thinking. But if you have never had such an opportunity, you can still do a perfectly good job of planning if you understand what it really means. You can define it by saying it is the process by which one learns to deal with life in the years to come, first by knowing as much as possible about what one can expect, next by finding out what can be attained, and finally by preparing for possible changes, some of which are forseeable.

The years ahead *can* be good, rich, and rewarding. At the least, they need not be empty. Many things that cause old age to be miserable are known, and some remedies have already been discovered. Many others that lead to a fully realizable goal, given the will, are also known. Happily, most of them depend not on legislation, nor on other people, but on oneself and one's own attitudes.

What Does Being "Old" Mean?

Whether you are forty or fifty years old and intend to take time by the forelock and start planning for the leisure you'll have in fifteen and twenty years, or whether you have waited till R-Day has almost arrived, there is one thing to do, even before you examine your financial assets or decide where you want to live. Planning for retirement does not mean starting off, like Don Quixote, in all directions at once. First of all, learn something about the process of aging; you'll find it considerably different from the picture that the average person conjures up so glibly.

There is no precise point when anybody enters the state of being an elderly sage, if he ever does, any more than there was a specific point when you ceased to be a young child and became an adolescent, or emerged from youth into maturity. You are not going to experience any discernible breaking point between middle and old age, any more than you will feel a difference in yourself the day before or the day after your retirement. Furthermore, there are vast differences among aging people—one person may act "old" when he is forty, or younger; another may have the zest and physical stamina of the eighty-year-old man who had a consuming passion for square dancing and indulged it weekly. That is, we not only all age differently but parts of our body—cells, organs, connective tissues, and so on— go through the aging process at different intervals within our own bodies, and do not necessarily resemble the speed of anybody else's.

A person who is a newcomer to the sixty-five plus group has much to learn. One important fact is that if you are in it now, or verging on it, you are of the generation exposed to more cultural, industrial, social, and economic changes than any previous generation knew, and your schooling and medical attention were probably different. It is likely you have the vigor of your parents when they were in the forty-five to fifty-five-year-old range, and ought to live like it.

What somebody has termed the "sixty-fifth birthday syndrome" is outmoded. The seventy-five-year-olds of 1970 are likely to look, act, and feel much younger than the sixty-five-year-olds of the 1880's. Thanks to lowered infant mortality and control of such former quick killers of the old, like pneumonia, you have at least a fifty-fifty chance of living a quarter-century beyond your sixty-fifth year.

Just what does this imposing array of statistics mean to you personally? A satisfying, happy old age is not going to come automatically; you may think you earned a comfortable retirement because you worked forty years or so, but perhaps you only earned a pension. The main question is, what are you really going to do with the years ahead? Life reduced to pursuit of the sun or even an interesting hobby sooner or later palls. The man or woman who recognizes this by the time he or she has to give up the thirty-five to forty-hour-a-week work routine is the one who is going to be able to continue as a functioning member of society. Studies made by the American Medical Association show that extending a vigorous life span calls for more than medications, and that a sense of purpose is as vital as adequate nutrition as one grows older.

Investment in Worthwhile Leisure

If you are not going to "rot" out your sixties and seventies, what are you going to do with all that free time?

People like Dr. Eveline M. Burns have found one answer. "No one knows from what she has really retired," said one of her colleagues. Officially, at sixty-seven, she became a professor emeritus at Columbia University's School of Social Work. But she still lectures; still is a consultant to city, state, Federal, and private commissions; and is often called on to make speeches and write articles.

"When you're so busy, you just don't quit," she says. However, it is her philosophy, not her capabilities, that other people would do well to emulate. Like many of us, Dr. Burns would like to change the world she lives in. "But," she remarks, "I never stop to ask myself if I am even making a dent. If the answer were 'no,' I would be too discouraged. You just go on, doing the best you can."

There is nothing inherent in this point of view which states it must be sparked by the government or an organization, national or local. Nor need it be confined to those with postgraduate degrees, or any degrees at all. Nor is it limited to one sex, or a particular social stratum.

There is no dearth of jobs that give meaning to life, however long, and a tremendous need for all types of people to do them. Everyone can make his own contribution, not necessarily by sticking to his last, but by finding the right place where his strength and ripe experience will count most, with or without pay.

There is great unrest in our contemporary world, but there is also greater opportunity to solve its problems in ways our immediate forefathers never dreamed of.

"I can't wait to begin!" This is what a sixty-year-old mechanic wrote when he applied to the Peace Corps. With more than thirty years of construction experience behind him, he was assigned to a road-building job in Tunisia.

They call out "Hi! Mom!" from their bed or their wheelchairs when a woman volunteer comes to a veterans' hospital near a great city. She travels there twice a week, fair weather or foul. For seven years she has been teaching photography. At Christmas time she takes photographs of all her "boys" and hand-colors them as her present to their families.

"When I was a girl," she says, "I was just a social butterfly. When I married I managed a large household and helped my husband in his business and in the rearing of five children. Now I've a chance to use a hobby I took up years ago so it really means something in the lives of other people."

It can be an exhilarating experience, as these two and many others have found, to arrive at the stage where one has earned the right to stop and take stock; to realize there is still time to enrich one's own life in ways and to an extent that may never have been possible before, but also to have the time and the energy to work for the ideas and the ideals one believes in. That is heady wine at any age.

Adjusting to Retirement

A good adjustment to retirement calls for redirection of one's talents and experience. It also requires a re-evaluation of ideas and attitudes formulated early in life and an honest appraisal to find out if they are obsolete or a hindrance to coming to grips with contemporary society. Frequently the acquisition of new information, new interests, and perhaps even new skills is called for. The latter may be used to increase financial resources or merely to broaden one's horizon. There is time at last to look into the possibilities of broadening a hobby, undertaking a community interest in depth, or even beginning or continuing studies for a college degree.

There is, in short, a necessity for purposeful activity during the years ahead when you will be free to forge your own pattern of living. If this includes something that will enrich the lives of others besides yourself and your family you will not have to be a genius like Titian, who painted great pictures in his nineties, to find that people within and without your immediate circle will dismiss your chronological age as of no importance.

When John W. Gardner was Secretary of Health, Education, and Welfare, he said that the nation, having made gains in improving pensions and making health care available to older people as their "right," ought to increase its efforts to conquer the problem of putting interest and purpose into the lives of the retired. He also said, "If the individual reaching retirement is fully alive and accustomed to thinking constructively about life's transitions, he will be far better fitted for the next stage of the journey."

One example will serve to illustrate the possibilities for people who believe that aging is synonymous with neither rust nor decay.

Dr. Lennig Sweet, a retired community leader in Denver, Colorado with a broad background in recreational, church, governmental, and overseas relief work, believed that far too few people know how to plan for their later years.

At the age of seventy-five Dr. Sweet put his ideas into action. He prepared a comprehensive syllabus, designed to prepare group leaders to conduct pre-retirement discussions for men and women still some years away from their own retirement. Training workshops were set up, and participants were chosen from a wide section of business and community organizations. The program was launched under the sponsorship of Denver's Adult Education Council, and funded through Colorado's Commission on the Aging. Dr. Sweet acted as part-time volunteer consultant.

The response was enthusiastic. Originally seventy group leaders were trained, and the number later increased to a hundred. They, in turn, went back to organizations and to industry to lead courses for pre-retirees in groups of approximately fifteen each. Where necessary, resource people supplemented discussions in such fields as living arrangements, health maintenance, financial planning, legal matters, family relationships, and so forth.

After its first successful year the cycle begun by Dr. Sweet had set a pattern that has spread in ever-widening circles. Several colleges and universities have incorporated the syllabus into their extension courses; other cities in Colorado followed Denver's example, and nearby states did the same. The Administration on Aging hopes the Denver pattern will be a prototype for the entire country. So the activity begun by one man in what most people would refer to as his old age has already borne rich results. And who can say which period of Dr. Sweet's busy life has been the most fruitful?

To Work or Not to Work

Many people, sadly, are unwilling to face the fact that in life, from infancy on, no role is ever static. Unable to come to grips with the fact that they must face change, they try to hang on to what they have. They cling to a position, a business, a profession—or their children—past the time when they ought to leave well enough alone. Or, if it is a job that leaves them at some retirement date, they make an attempt—sometimes frantic, often futile—to find another, whether or not it is really financially necessary.

Anyone who still has a choice of crossroads—preferably before he reaches it—should stop where he is to find out exactly what work, especially the kind that has become a habit over the years, really means to him. This is true whether one is fifty or seventy, a housewife or a bank president.

If you are eager to keep on using what you know and all the experinece that gave you the chance to learn what neophytes in your field are still ignorant of, you will be honest with yourself in posing questions that require no professional counseling to solve. In general, most of us need to answer frankly, at least to ourselves, queries like these:

Is it necessary for me to have work that brings in a financial return? If so, how much?

Can I get equal satisfaction by continuing to do something else that yields a lesser income—or none at all?

Do I want to continue to work for love of the work itself, or because it gives me a chance to prove I'm still capable?

Do I believe working for monetary compensation has some inherent good in it, and working without pay a poor substitute?

Do I still have the ability to manage people or affairs, make accurate judgments, create new ideas?

Do I need to be paid a wage commensurate with my wisdom, or will I be satisfied to do a job without pay that will right some wrongs?

Anyone can come to his own conclusions. That is, he can if he does not start out with the distorted view that all that lies ahead is a twilight period. There is work, real work, he can do anywhere, at any age. No one in our complex society need echo the ancient Chinese poet who said that he solaced himself by playing the harp and reading books "to forget the lost cap of office."

The word "employment," it is true, has different meanings for different individuals. To one it means full-time remunerative work and nothing else; for another it is a part-time job taken merely to supplement a pension; for still another it means work that makes his hometown a good place to live in, and he may or may not be paid for doing it. For a minority, it means a place to go every day without necessitating a break in long-established routine.

Before you ask yourself in which category you belong, remember that paid work is simply and strictly a function of labor supply. This applies just as much to medical practice or teaching as it does to factory work. When labor is scarce in every field—such as in wartime—even the very old are hired to take up the slack. When labor is abundant—young labor, that is—it is a different matter. The problem of finding work, furthermore, may not be one of physical aging at all, but rather of technological obsolescence, which can take place after a couple of decades of work in a specific field.

But if you are asking, "What can I do when I reach my own sixties or seventies, if I want to go on being employed?" the answer is that there is no natural law that says that any person is incapable of doing a full day's work on a specific day. There are people like the Reverend John Kuhn. He worked for more than thirty-five years for Western Electric, and during the last four or five studied for the ministry in addition. He assumed the first pastorate he ever had had the same year he retired.

There are also people like Louis B. Deitz, who at seventy-six entered his second post-retirement career—but this time as a volunteer. After years of working for one company as a metalurgical engineer, he retired, and then worked eight years more for another as a technical advisor. Finally he took an assignment—without pay —as a consultant to a smelting company in Turkey.

These are people who do not think of themselves as extraordinary, any more than Mrs. F. M. Barry of Milwaukee, Wisconsin, did, when she was honored at ninety-one as a still active volunteer for the American Red Cross. All three illustrate Thomas Carlyle's dictum. He wrote, "Blessed is he who has found his work. Let him ask no other blessedness." He said nothing about being paid for it.

But if you do rebel against the idea of being cut off from your office or factory job at the age of sixty-five or even less, remember that the figure is purely arbitrary. Sixty-five as the usual dividing line between work and retirement came into existence when Social Security program became part of our legislation during the depression decade of the thirties. It was accepted as the age for mandatory retirement in the occupations covered by the law partly because we followed the European systems (which laid down that age as the Rubicon for the first time in 1879!). A second major reason was the fact that it was believed the new social security benefits would induce older people to leave the labor market at this time of great national unemployment. Subsequently private business took social security benefits into consideration when they formed their own pension systems and used the same chronological date. But today, retirement ages, sparked by automation, labor unions, and a mounting population, are going steadily downward.

Once you realize these facts you may not look more jaunty or act differently but you will understand why the U.S. Employment Service and its affiliated state offices often have special representatives who concentrate on convincing employers that capable people, regardless of age, are worth hiring. (If you need or want a job in any field for pay this is a good place to start your search.)

What Leaving Work Means

Most economists think the generation coming to maturity now will take for granted shorter work weeks, longer holidays and earlier retirement in a world where work for pay will not be considered the only good. Yet anyone who grew up in the first half of this century knows that we are still not only a youth-dominated society, but a work-oriented one. We are all strongly influenced by the still prevalent Puritan ethic, which equates work for pay—preferably hard work—with moral virtues, and success in business or in a profession with well-being. This is probably a major reason why there is a built-in prejudice against the idea of retirement in most of us.

On the other hand, it is not necessary to aim at dying with your boots on if you have never liked the boots in the first place, or if they have become uncomfortable or worn out.

Just what will you miss if you leave a profession, cease to operate a business, or quit a job, and what can take its place?

A foremost authority in labor relations sums it up in this way:

"People mourn the feeling of accomplishment that comes from a job well done, whether it's sweeping a floor or presiding at a committee or board meeting. If there is no time-clock, literally or figuratively, to punch, they're afraid their days of usefulness are over. And," he added, "everybody would like to hang on to the values work brings to most of us—independence, recognition, fellowship, status at home and in the community. What we all have to do is to buck that many-faceted myth which says that work for compensation is the only way to get them."

31

Easing the Way to New Values

Some people find great satisfaction in pursuing a second career in a field where they are greatly needed, even if they earn a lesser income. Hastings College in California is one institution that has taken advantage of rigid retirement rules in other institutions of higher learning. Its law faculty is made up of retired professors, many of whom had already won distinction elsewhere. The so-called shortage occupations—teaching, the health field, social work—all beckon, particularly to those who have long served in the same vineyard. Physicians and medical technicians of all kinds are sought by organizations that will gladly take them on part-time or for short periods, here or abroad, for expenses or a little more. Lawyers, like old soldiers, need never die professionally as long as such groups as the legal aid societies and the poor exist. Retired foremen, like retired bookkeepers, gardeners, bank cashiers, housekeepers—in fact the whole gamut of American labor—find they are wanted and can be used in the semi-voluntary capacities offered by one or another of the domestic versions of the Peace Corps.

Yet even if one can hang onto his usual job or stay in a profession well beyond the ordinary period, sooner or later he will have to make way for new blood, new ideas, new ways, and the younger generation pressing up from below. Then there comes a period of adjustment. This is true for everybody, whether he officially has retired at a mandatory date or prolonged the going for a while. This is the "moment of truth." Because no matter how much one has chafed against routine and responsibility at home or abroad, and sighed for the time when he would be his own master, when the day does approach the prospect may seem a little less pleasing.

This is normal and ought not to dismay anybody. If plans for prolonged vacations, for pursuit of an old hobby, for new studies, do not seem enough to fill the new leisure time, increased by thirty-five to forty hours a week, that, too, is normal. Retirement, like any other phase of existence, requires time for adaptation.

Unless you want to end as "Chairman of the Bored," to use Edward Streeter's significant, witty phrase, this is the time for exploration, for finding out what has really been happening since your own goals were set in early maturity. It is the time to decide—if you do not want to hold yourself completely aloof from your younger contemporaries and from society, however turbulent—whether you, too, ought not to take a hand in shaping it.

Finding a Suitable Goal

In recent years both the Executive and the Congressional branches of government have given official recognition to the fact that the qualities possessed by a generation to whom a good job of work was always a matter of pride are still needed in our country. There is also a growing, if sometimes slow, conviction that older men and women are ready and willing to help others when they are permitted to do it, and to help themselves when they are given the chance.

This new breath blowing through governmental circles is clearly defined in the language that created a Senate Subcommittee on Retirement and the Individual. It authorizes the Committee to make inquiries and to report on "the institution of retirement and its impact on the individual, especially as regards the problem of adjusting to a new role in life . . . and his need for meaning and fulfillment in the retirement years . . . so that loss of job and job status will not be a demoralizing and deteriorative experience."

There you have it clearly spelled out for you! But how are you going to find a compelling goal or a purposeful activity that will fit this new role and your own strengths? Of course there can be no categorical answer that will fit everybody. You may be able to find your own solution in pursuing something that has long beckoned. Or you may want to continue a pursuit in leisure that you had to undertake formerly under pressure of time. Or you may need a space of weeks or months to become involved in community affairs, or to allow the community to realize you have strengths to offer. You do not have to carve out a major goal for it to be a good one.

"You're lucky if you can say to yourself, 'Now's the time I can do something I've really wanted to do!' "

The speaker was a man in his sixties, formerly a storekeeper in a Northern city in a far from affluent neighborhood. When a heart attack forced him to slow down, he decided to give up his business and spend his time fighting against the things he did not like. The way he chose was to give shelter and board, with the aid and consent of his wife, to two, three, occasionally four boys and girls. Usually they are sharecroppers' children, black or white, from the state in which he was born. The apartment is modest and there is only one spare bedroom. Two boys stayed all one winter while they went to trade schools, but the majority of the young people come for two weeks at a time in the summer. One is now a "permanent" boarder till he finishes working his way through college. The "foster parents" have no children of their own.

A major decision like this is not made hastily. Arriving at the age of sixty-five—or seventy-five—does not automatically confer wisdom. But everyone has the right, even the obligation, to see that whatever talents he has and whatever life has taught him about how to use them, do not fall into innocuous disuse through neglect.

There is little evidence to prove that it is only youth, or great leaders—though both are valuable—who make a better world. Every one of us, at every stage of life, has a contribution he can make. In the long run it is the small talents of many people of all ages who harness their strengths together which bring about changes that alter the face of things for the better.

If you say to yourself, "What can I do at my age?" and do nothing, you are going to be a failure. People need to feel they *can* do something, before any success, big or small, can be achieved. Without a goal that gives relevance, significance, and usefulness, late life, like years at any stage in existence, can become drab and humdrum.

There are small jobs to be done in your immediate neighborhood, and there are other, more difficult jobs to be done there or elsewhere. There are in this world, before it becomes a fit place for all to live in, tasks so enormous that they are impossible for any one person to see completed in his own lifetime. And there are other jobs, equally important, at which you can chip away with your fellows till perhaps you can see some solutions take form which never existed before. Finally, there is still other work to be done, which can be accomplished by one individual, even if he works alone.

The thing to do is to find the one particular role one wants to play that will fully use the capacities inborn and those developed over the years. A motive for action in late life, as in earlier years, needs to be sincere, deeply felt. Once that has been determined there is no longer any question that the word "retirement" will carry a bad connotation. It means time for constructive citizenship; it can be the means of achieving a happy, full life. And as William James, the philosopher, once said, "The great use of life is to spend it for something that will outlast it."

Chapter II

What Can You Do?

Several centuries ago Edmund Burke made an observation that is worth recalling: "For the triumph of evil, it is only necessary for good people to do nothing." Burke's concern was not with what could or could not be done during this or that period of life, but what could be accomplished by exercising the nobler impulses of man.

It is much easier for all of us to sigh over the evils at City Hall, to mourn that certain children are denied opportunities that all boys and girls should enjoy, to accept the fact that there has always been saber-rattling around the world, than to give the energy, patience, and optimism needed to overcome these or other crises which arise each day. Yet if you hold the American attitude that problems are inescapable, but not necessarily unsolvable, you will want to do more than wish uneasily in a vague way that you could "do something."

Granted that the power to see what is not before your eyes is very difficult in a society as large, impersonal, and massive as ours. Yet this is what is needed. You need to see in imagination the wretched condition that many millions of people in America face, often within blocks of opulence. You need to see in imagination also the conditions that confront other wretched millions elsewhere in the world.

For those conditions, if permitted to continue, will destroy most of what you prize in the world you are leaving to your children.

In this country there are thousands of societies and organizations, all products of voluntary action local, national, and international in scope. They are a means through which any person of goodwill at any age who has a latent desire to leave "footprints on the sands of time" can work. They represent a means through which all Americans can demonstrate ability to better their surroundings or that of their neighbors without violent revolution, and contribute to the betterment of the United States as a whole, and to mankind everywhere.

Why People Volunteer

What motivates people to volunteer their services at any time of life is likely to represent a combination of many reasons. At times the humanitarian feeling may be based on a strong religious motive; at others on the compassionate fear that "There, but for the grace of God, go I!" In the best of us it can represent a conscious or unconscious need for recognition and status in the family or the community. At all times when we volunteer we are searching not only to give greater meaning to our own life, but to justify the ways of American democracy.

A steady stream of letters and telephone calls came into the New York office of the National Council of Jewish Women when a newspaper article announced the formation of the Council's Senior Service Corps. Requests for more information poured in from every type of retired individual. One thread ran through all the queries— rebellion against enforced and empty idleness.

If you find a useful role to play you too will certainly avoid loneliness, boredom, and frustration—the three evils commonly associated with growing older. In its "Design for Action" manual, the Massachusetts Commission on Aging outlines a whole series of possibilities for the person who realizes there is great satisfaction in offering what the psychologists term a "positive image" of an alert person with still useful talents who can meet a genuine manpower need in our country. As the Commission says in its Manual,

Voluntary work serves a double purpose—it restores to older people some of the value and satisfactions of a former job and it makes available an abundance of their talents and skills to supplement the often inadequate staffs of community agencies.

The Enjoyment of Leisure

The unthinking—usually the young, still harried by problems of child-rearing, earning, and planning an uncertain future in a competitive world—often ask, "Why do people volunteer when they have the right to rest, to do exactly what they choose for the rest of their lives?"

The answer, of course, is that enjoyment of leisure is not a synonym for idleness. Nor does it necessarily mean more ceramic-making or more trips to vacation spots, though it may include these good things. It means exercising the right and the responsibility to invest time in becoming involved in what is going on around you, not only for the sake of society, but for yourself.

Howard Bede, a successful advertising executive, threw himself with ardor into working with schoolchildren on a volunteer basis, and then became active in attracting others throughout Illinois to do the same thing. When he was asked why he devoted so much time and thought to work he had never done before, this was his answer: "I left my advertising work with a sense of regret and some misgivings. But I couldn't shut off my energy and creative thinking any more than a stream could suddenly stop flowing at a given point. I wanted to go on being active, doing things that were worthwhile, *meaning* something."

The late Eduard C. Lindeman, distinguished philosopher, teacher, scholar, and social reformer, gave the same answer in a different form. Once, when he was lecturing on citizen participation, Dr. Lindeman said this: "The act of volunteering is an assertion of individual worth. The person who of his own free will decides to work on behalf of the good of his community is in effect saying, 'I have gifts and talents which are needed. I am a person who accepts a responsibility, not because it is imposed upon me, but rather because I wish to be useful. My right to be thus used is a symbol of my personal dignity and worth!'"

Dr. Lindeman said this more than two decades ago, but it is even more relevant now when so many aspects of American life are being questioned and re-evaluated. This is a time when the young are obsessed by a mission to purge themselves, their parents, and their society. But it is also clearly a time that demands involvement of all of us of every age, and in particular those who have the time and experience that fit them to be, in some ways, their brothers' keepers.

Today's Opportunities Are Greater

There are not only more and different kinds of services one can engage in than there were in your parents' day, but a great many new ways to give them.

To encounter an eighty-two-year-old former professor of French conducting classes for adults on a nondenominational basis in her church is new. To use the talents of an electronics engineer to open up new horizons to a high-school generation with the use of slides and moving pictures compiled in thirty or more years of experience is also a departure from old-time school ways. But, after all, both acts are simply extensions of the once-prevalent role of the grandparent in the home circle.

While volunteering of any kind still means giving time and effort, one's pocketbook may not always be as big as one's heart, so the word "volunteering" is going through some interesting variations. In some fields, men and women may not receive a regular wage, but they are reimbursed for living expenses (as in VISTA, the domestic Peace Corps) and have something added in a lump sum at the end of their service. It does not add up to a regular salary, but it does allow them to make a contribution without personal hardship. Other agencies are coming around to the point of view that car fares, lunch money, and even uniforms, if they have to be worn, are a small expenditure to give to men and women who are doing work that otherwise might not be done at all.

No one need be a martyr to communal responsibility. "I've waited thirty-five years to have more time to do the kind of weaving my grandmother taught me!" one woman, herself a grandmother, said. But in addition to weaving, this ex-housewife has organized an arts and crafts program in a neighborhood settlement that attracts children in Harlem every day in the week.

Must recreational pursuits or hobbies be abandoned? Must golf or swimming or traveling to far climes be ruled out in favor of more serious missions? The answer, obviously, is a resounding no! But it is wise for those no longer heedless and young to view the pursuit of pleasure in its proper perspective. Shuffleboard games or bridge can be amusing, but only when they are recreational interludes. One may gratify himself with a clear conscience if he picks up the fiddle he had to drop when he got immersed in rising to the top, or polishes his game of tennis, or fulfills a long postponed desire to try his hand at painting or wood-carving or astronomy, but none of them can be the basis for a solid, satisfying legacy laid down for the years ahead. There has to be something more than self-gratification.

It is just this challenge in retirement that leaves each individual free to forge his own pattern of living. Those who drift then, as at any other time of life, pay the consequences.

"It does no good to worry in advance," was one woman's answer, which she considered philosophic. But the married daughter she was planning to descend on in a distant city was worrying about it. "What will mother do while I'm at work, or if my husband and I want to go out in the evening together?" she asked.

And what about the widower who since his wife's death has been puttering about his garden? Is he merely going to grow more and more vegetables and let more dishes pile up till his weekly maid-of-all-work arrives? And more important, is he going to become more and more hostile when the neighbor's children volley their ball over the fence and it hits his prize cabbages?

How to Begin

Opportunities abound, and so do good causes. There are small jobs for those with limited capacities or time or strength. There are bigger jobs waiting for those with the energy and desire to carry them out. The feeling of meaning and usefulness is encouraged by physicians because they say it delays the aging process and helps maintain optimal health. Social agencies are increasingly concerned with developing channels to use the growing reservoir of latent talents and increased leisure time created by retirees with a healthy outlook and good stamina. "Senior citizens' centers" now prefer to be called multipurpose centers and place more emphasis on community involvement programs than they used to.

Knowing all this is one thing, and implementing it another. Where and how does one begin? No one need feel helpless, even in the face of social problems of our period.

The starting place has to be the realization that you cannot solve everything you see that you feel is wrong, and quite possibly you will not be able to do as much as you would have earlier in life, given the same amount of time to spend. But you can do *something.* A good rule of thumb is one that was often cited by Eleanor Roosevelt. She said that since no one could solve all the social problems— even in his own community, much less those of the world—the best thing to do is to find one thing that is absorbing and interesting, within and without one's own personal circle. In this way one can satisfy his own needs and accomplish something for others.

For some this would mean active participation in cultural areas to help assure the continuance of the arts in one's hometown, perhaps a renewal or strengthening of interest of earlier years. For others it would mean greater participation and an offer to take on more responsibility in some worthy civic or philanthropic endeavor.

The task for anyone no longer compelled to concentrate on moneymaking or career-making or family-raising is to find a specific area where he can concentrate rather than disperse his energies. If he can make an investment of himself, as Mr. Hunter did, which will outlast his own time, he is lucky indeed.

In December, 1965, the National Association of Social Workers voted a special citation to eighty-two-year-old Joel Du Bois Hunter. In 1946 he had retired as General Superintendent of the United Charities of Chicago. The citation read:

> For his second retirement career in volunteer service, leading to the establishment of much needed mental health and social welfare services in Clearwater, Florida, and adding further lustre to the distinguished professional contributions he had made to social work and social welfare over the years.

It Takes More than Money

Many say that the world's biggest heart, measured by generosity, belongs to Americans, who annually give over ten billion dollars— an average of fifty dollars each from every man, woman, and child in the United States—to good causes. But money is by no means the only criterion of unselfishness.

Everybody can take time to do something, not only those living on a large income, but even those who have a minimal one, or lack robust health. Mrs. Summers is a woman now in her seventies who has a heart ailment that keeps her housebound much of the time. She learned Braille, however, so she could help blind children learn to read. In her town a social agency sends boys and girls to her not only to study but to enjoy the games and treats she lovingly prepares for them.

Mrs. Summers has to work as an individual, but more often satisfaction is gained in being part of a joint effort. Quite often there are opportunities to meet people with ideals and ideas similar to your own. And these associations (which even in late life can produce friendships) based on shared interests, have a depth and quality not always found in the social relationships of everyday life.

Directly after World War II it was calculated that over 30,000,000 people were giving unpaid help to religious, social, political, and civic organizations. Since then the number has swelled by many more millions.

Unless one is endowed with great talent or great wealth, or both, he will usually accomplish more as an active member of a group than as a lone wolf. But if you can find none that seems exactly to suit you, then take the initiative, seek those who are like-minded, and form one. If there are problems in your community that you think are not being met, it is hardly likely that you will be the only person in town who thinks so. Whether you make your impact by taking part in or originating a better race relations program, or working for better understanding between labor and management, or harnessing all your talents to getting better schools, or in something else, a beginning of your search can be found in Dr. Albert Schweitzer's words. "Open your eyes," he said, "and look for some work for the sake of men, which needs a little time, a little friendship, a little sympathy, a little toil."

What Needs to Be Done

Begin with something specific. If you are not already known as a tireless and effective volunteer, ask yourself if you are willing to work your way up, as you would have to do in any business or a profession. Or are you demanding that you be put somewhere near the top on the basis of what you have accomplished already in life?

Once you come to terms with yourself, there is a wide choice of outlets for you, depending on whether you can do your best work organizing or planning or writing, keeping accounts and records, dealing with people, making speeches—or any or all combinations of the many types of work that need to be done for undermanned or underfinanced organizations.

If you have money to spare there are a thousand good causes existing on a shoestring for which you could raise or contribute funds.

If you want to do your work through your church on a more personal basis you can lead a discussion class or a social problems group or help out in a summer camp or at a reception desk.

If you want to improve international relations, join a study group and when you know enough, throw yourself into work with other men and women who want to achieve the same ends.

If it is the evils of poverty and city ghettos that move you most, there is plenty of room for those figuratively or literally willing to roll up their sleeves.

If you want to learn how to use what you know or how to talk and move people to action, you can equip yourself by participating in adult education classes. That movement itself—popularly known as "continuing education"—may give you a lifelong occupation even if you do no more than keep informed of the depths of our social inadequacies and raise your voice to combat them when the occasion is opportune.

If good race relations seems the most burning issue where you live, sometimes one word to your neighbors, a letter to an editor, a speech at a club meeting, will help bring a whole community's attention to a project that needs aid.

If you feel there is something rotten in politics, maybe you ought to get into the fray yourself. Join the local club of a political party and help interest your neighbors. This is a chore only until you get to know the individuals so that you can exchange views with them. Do not stop there. Make your voice felt nationally by keeping close watch on what your representatives in Congress are doing. Even if you are housebound you can still write letters to them or to your state legislators to let them know what you think they should do on this or that question affecting you and your fellow citizens.

If you are interested in your peers, why not concentrate on problems of the aging population in your area? If there is no multipurpose center open to them, or no local council on aging, work to get them established so their interests (and yours) will be protected.

If you have never before been a "joiner" there is no better time than your retirement years to begin to ally yourself with some group that stands for the things you believe in, whether it is a committee of your neighborhood center, a social action group, a trade union with a program for the underdog, or the local museum or orchestra trying to keep afloat.

Any intelligent citizen, in short, can help solve some of the problems that the jet and atomic age has brought. Never doubt that the wisdom of your years and the work of your hands is needed. No matter how much governmental or state aid there is now or to come, there will always be a gap to be filled by those who can provide individual strength, community support, and personal service. Your share may be anything from giving a few words of informal counseling to troubled youngsters, to the imaginative job that spurs laggard public opinion to undertake needed parks or playgrounds or to demolish firetrap housing.

Some people have special skills grown rusty through disuse; but they can be refurbished. Others learn new ones through which they can give expression to what they believe in.

Range of Activities Is Wide

The scope of possible activities anywhere is wide enough to suit anybody. For example, the Volunteer Bureau of Sacramento, California, addressed its recruitment flyer to those "who want to help with many interesting kinds of volunteer work in seventy-five non-profit health, welfare, educational, and cultural agencies." It invited those "who have a morning, an afternoon, an evening time once a week or now and then" to volunteer to work in "libraries, day camps, museums, hospitals, playgrounds, nurseries, offices, recreation centers, schools."

Here is their list, typical of those elsewhere; the opportunities are given in alphabetical order.

Assist in recreational programs
Act as a receptionist
Befriend the mentally ill
Be a friendly visitor
Drive the handicapped
File
Fold, stuff, stamp envelopes
Give information
Hand-address

Instruct in arts, crafts, music
Mimeograph
Open and sort mail
Photograph or type
Use your hobbies for others
Work with children or adults
Work with senior citizens
Write publicity

In a more formal way, the posts that need to be filled in any city in the United States can be summed up under these headings:

Civic education. This is a wide area for anyone who wants to make a contribution by writing or illustrating informative pamphlets, giving personal instruction, doing interviewing, and doorbell ringing for good causes, manning information booths, doing public speaking, planning, designing, or helping build exhibits or other types of visual displays. The ultimate aim of each is to stimulate the general public to become informed and vocal on topics vital to the general welfare of themselves and others.

Cultural activities. The word loosely covers what is done in museums, through public forums, libraries, educational exhibits for children or adults, and nonprofit magazines, or in radio and television hours. Volunteers help by aiding museum curators, becoming instructors or lecturers, leading community forums, preparing posters or guides, handling publicity, acting as guides to individuals or groups, ushering, and so forth.

Health and medical fields. Hospitals, clinics, and all types of institutions need laboratory or ward aides, book distributors, transportation aid for invalids, entertainers, receptionists, personal aid to patients, and "friendly visitors" for a variety of purposes.

Office work. This is a perennial necessity in many kinds of civic organizations. It offers a useful outlet for those with no professional or technical background, for people who want to work in short-term campaigns, or for those who prefer routine jobs that require no great intellectual investment. The general term "office work" covers all the usual types from stenography to stamping letters.

Political work. This is perhaps the area most relegated to the background by retirees, yet it is a neglected field in which men and women (of any age) who care about good government can put their shoulders to the wheel in the hope of helping themselves and their fellow citizens and those who come after them. The range of possible activities is wide enough to suit anybody. You can work either for the party of your choice, or on a non-partisan basis in any city in the land. Unpaid jobs open to all: telephoning; doorbell ringing; transporting laggard potential voters; serving on study committees, in voters' leagues, on taxpayers' associations, neighborhood improvement associations; and preparing mailings time and again.

If anybody needs inspiration he can get it from the story of Dr. Ethel Percy Andrus. When Dr. Andrus retired as the first woman principal of a California high school she determined to do something that would give older Americans a chance to help solve their own problems. The organization she founded was the National Retired Teachers Association, and later, a sister body, the American Association for Retired Persons. Both of them have a variety of programs. But two decades later, she described their varied purposes as "Putting spunk into those who need to get their lives moving again!"

Advantages on the Side of Age

There are certain advantages in having time on your side. You can be more judicial, more altruistic in your approach than can persons tied to the necessity of economic gain or advancement in a profession. "Intelligence and reflection and judgment reside in old men, and if there had been none of them no state could exist at all," said that great Roman, Cicero, some twenty centuries ago.

If you have any doubts that you can make your views felt on a national question, or that you will face difficulty if you try to amend a bad local situation, remember Clara Barton. She founded the American National Red Cross when she was past sixty and served it for twenty-two years. When she resigned at eighty-three she founded another association of civic importance and served as its President until she was ninety-one.

One does not have to aspire to such greatness to make a genuine contribution to society in his later years. Some scientists of repute believe that eventually the normal life span of civilized man will be around a hundred and fifty years. This promises a thrilling future for the race, only if we can succeed in adding meaning to the lengthening years. One does not have to believe in Utopia, or to wait for the millennium to begin, or shrug off responsibilities by saying "Oh, I'm too old now to begin!" The artist Shalom, whose work UNICEF used for a holiday greeting card, did not begin to paint till he was almost sixty-five. Richard Welling, a New York lawyer, did not think he was too old in his eighties to chair a national committee concerned with stimulating better student self-government.

The list of other useful older citizens throughout the country is already long. It will be much longer when more and more older men and women discover there are many fronts on which they can battle. All that is needed is a little effort to uncover them, hope in the future of our country, and belief that you, too, can help shape that future at any age.

Rabbi Hillel, who lived in the first century before Jesus Christ, stated the issue for all of us for all time:

If I am not for myself, who will be for me?
But if I care for myself only, what am I?
And if not now, when?

Chapter III

Opening Doors
to Civic Opportunity

"Older Americans have skills, experience, and wisdom which they need to use and which the nation needs." This is what President Johnson said when he established the Administration on Aging in 1965.

Nowhere can this truism be fulfilled better than in the complex urban community of today where sociologists refer to the loss of relationship with one's surroundings as "the disease of anonymous isolation."

A major reason why cities are not better places to live in—as has been said many times—lies in the fact too few people take the time and make the effort to better them. For it is no copybook maxim to say that if you want to lend years of genuine social worth you can do it in any urban setting, whether it is the one you grew up in or the one you moved to in later years, or even in the sunny climes that may claim only a part of your time.

One of the redeeming features of any metropolis is the fact that it gives its residents an infinite variety of choices in everything. This applies to good causes as well as cultural events. As a California Volunteer Service Bureau pointed out, "Utilization of volunteers has moved from the desirable to the necessary, if citizen-focused health, education, and welfare programs are to maintain their tempo of service in the community."

The gamut of what is open to you can run from the boards and committees on which elder sages have always had a chance to sit, to organizing a puppet show in a neighborhood center or writing letters for hospitalized veterans. You can decide whether you want to work alone, with your own age group, or as a member of the concerned public of varying ages. You can offer to lend a helping hand to some local organization trying to expand, or one that is trying to bring a program into your city that never existed there before.

If you become one of that stream of people who seek equable climes and a more leisurely pace, there is no quicker way to become part of your surroundings, and to make acquaintances who can ripen into worthwhile friends, than to seek outlets where you can help solve local problems. You may even be able to bring fresh solutions to bear on them simply because you are a newcomer, for long-standing ills often become so familiar to those who live among them they are accepted with resignation or semi-blindness.

In short, your legitimate goal is to find the niche into which you— not somebody else you admire—fit best. Whatever it is, its ultimate end will give you the greatest satisfaction if it revitalizes the old American tradition of neighbor helping neighbor which has suffered so greatly from the compartmentalization of urban living.

Rule #1: Like What You Do

How are you going to find the key that will open the door to just the opportunity you want, which, in turn, needs you? There are some basic rules, and the first one is to take your time. If you are planning for retirement or are already in it, you have enough leisure ahead of you to take a long look ahead and be sure before you rush into something that tempts you to believe that it is the right one for you. Your contributions do not need to be spectacular, but they do need to be useful. It costs money and time to prepare volunteers to work. Any professionally trained person looks with a jaundiced eye on would-be "do-gooders" who flit from one organization to another.

To look for something you will enjoy is a duty as well as a right. You also have a right to expect to be taken seriously and given work to do which stretches your capacities. But this is a *quid pro quo* proposition. If you let yourself be stampeded into something that may be well worth doing by someone else, not you; or show up reluctantly after you begin, with hesitation or doubts; or come a few times, decide you have made a mistake, and then leave, perhaps just at the point where a busy staff member thinks you *may* be of some help, then you have cost that agency more than you were ever worth. If you follow that practice more than once you will probably be giving a black name to others who may want to come after you and might do a better job. However, it is no reflection on you to say you will try out something and keep on with it if you can do it and it suits your needs and the organization's; just be sure that your point of view is understood.

Rule #2: Have Confidence in Yourself

No matter how limited specific techniques may be, a good volunteer should feel he is doing something worthwhile, but at the same time he should resist pressure to undertake something that he is not sure will hold his interest, or for which he has no talent. Take it for granted you can find something that gratifies you in this period of expanding and changing social services under both public and private auspices. In the so-called helping professions (social work, psychology, nursing, medicine, and so on) volunteers are always desperately needed to supplement the work of too few professional people.

Your motives need not be suspect. In one of New York City's busiest hospitals the director of volunteer services is one of many the country over who recognizes that people donate time and effort for a variety of reasons.

"Some of them say they want to help, to do something worthwhile with their free time," she says. "Others say it makes them feel 'good,' and still others quite candidly admit they have nothing else to do to fill up empty hours."

Yet in what is reputedly tagged as the coldest-hearted city in the world, a staggering total of more than a quarter-million New Yorkers give time and service to public and private schools, to the park system's betterment, to many types of social reform, and a variety of institutions. At the end of what is regarded as a typical twelve-month period, New York City's United Hospital Fund reported that 21,179 men and women had contributed almost 2.5 million hours to its member hospitals. The proof that many like what they do, and that that number includes the retired, can be found in a number of instances, of which these two are typical:

Mrs. Fanny J. is a retired milliner who walks twenty blocks from her home, to and from a hospital in Queens, New York, two or sometimes three days each week. "Why not?" she asks. "I like to walk. I'm all alone at home and I've nothing better to do. "And she adds, "I like to help sick people!" Mrs. J. helps by working in the linen room, mending sheets.

Peter J. puts the matter even more candidly. He is a retired fireman, and he does clerical work in the business office of a Manhattan hospital. "I could do fire prevention work on a voluntary basis," he says, "but I felt I had 'had it' after thirty-six years in the Department. Here they can't thank me enough for the little I do. I don't want to be thanked because it's something I do because I feel good about it; besides, it keeps me occupied!"

Rule #3: Find Out What Is Available

Start your own search by learning to know your city well, however large or small it is, and however long you have lived there. Do not rely on "what used to be." The most typical characteristic of our time is change. You will probably be surprised if you listen to the radio or look at television or read newspapers with the purpose of (a) finding out what is being done in the way of social action, and which organizations are engaged in it and who the individual leaders are; (b) discovering what the most forward-looking people in your city believe needs to be done to make it a better hometown for everybody; (c) listing the existing resources, and jotting down their plans for expanding or otherwise, and how they will meet community gaps.

If you have done your homework well you will then be able to select the agencies you would like to be a part of, provided of course you have been honest in assaying your qualifications to give aid to any one of them.

Before you get lost in the multiplicity of things you would like to do or see done, remind yourself of two salient facts. The first is that today's society makes use of an ever-increasing number of unsalaried helpers. Practically any metropolis would be able to match the West coast city whose central volunteer bureau listed six hundred openings in affiliated agencies as the norm for one month.

The second fact is the ground on which most people meet their Waterloo—the failure to take the job of volunteering seriously enough before they begin. You ought to be willing to give as much thought to finding your own particular role as you have given to any other important choice in your life, because this one will have a great deal to do with making the later years—short or long—rich and fruitful.

Judging One's Own Capacities

It is always good to know what one's assets are in relation to the value others put on them, and never more so than in volunteering. If you are in good health and have some special talents, you will be in demand. If you have never had time to give to public service before and have no special skills, or are not interested in using those you have, you will have to be content with doing such tasks as stapling reports or taking telephone messages, but you will be no less useful. You may bridle at the idea of being put to work sealing and stamping envelopes in a fund-raising campaign to which you yourself have been an annual contributor, but that simple bit of help in an under-staffed office may release a more technically knowledgeable person for an agency job that you cannot do.

Before you say a hurried "yes" or a too reluctant "no," save yourself disappointments and other people's time by making your own personal inventory (preferably in writing). It may be an eye-opener, or not, but it will certainly give you a clear indication of where to go for what you want to do.

To use the technical language of the welfare specialists, your choice should be predicated on intellectual and emotional interests. Translated into everyday terms, that means knowing answers to questions like these and being honest in your self-evaluation.

Do you like children and do you know how to play constructively with them? Or tutor them?

Or do you prefer being with adults? Can you work well with people younger or older than yourself?

Are you good at collecting data through personal interviews or doing research in libraries?

Do you prefer to present new ideas through the spoken word? Do you ever suffer from stage fright?

Would you like to try to sway people by what you write, or edit, with or without a by-line?

Do you get along well by yourself, or do you function better with a group?

What interests you most: the troubles of people in your own age group, teen-age conflicts, insufficient medical facilities, the drug problem, slum clearance, or some other deficiency in urban life?

Do not fall into the error of thinking that what you can do depends on how old you are. There are still staff members skeptical of the ability and willingness of a sixty or seventy-year-old to plunge through snow, or alternatively, face a hot summer sun to do regularly and faithfully a job he does not get paid for, but their number is diminishing. There are many who realize that formerly all services that affected community life were the domain of the volunteer, and that not all of them were young. By and large, it can be said categorically that once you have decided you want to participate in life, neither the calendar nor your impairments should hold you back.

"I am past seventy and have recently lost my sight, but I still ponder that old question, What can I do?" a woman had her granddaughter write the American Friends Service Committee. "I do not believe war and violence is ever a solution to any problem," she continued, "so I send for books and speeches you publish to give my friends."

In Chicago Mrs. Anna Jorgenson was recruited at eighty-four to demonstrate the art of spinning yarn for fourth-grade students at the Brook Park School. They were thrilled to find out she was using a one-hundred-and-fifty-year-old spinning wheel that had been on exhibit at the 1933 Century of Progress Fair in their city.

It can be said categorically that anyone who has lived fifty, sixty, or more years, has acquired some experience, or some ability, or has some native talent that can be put to use for somebody else's good.

Nevertheless, this does not mean you can always do just what you prefer; the mark of a really useful person (with or without pay) is the degree to which he can tolerate new ideas and be willing to undertake new experiences, and not continually hark back to old ones. (Isn't having the chance to open new doors for oneself one of the good reasons why one volunteers, and perfectly compatible with seeing that others are opened for his less fortunate neighbors?)

Personal Factors to Consider

The kind of person who comes to a busy agency and says (no doubt with passion, and means it) "I'll do anything!" is likely to leave his vis-à-vis considerably in doubt of his abilities, if not his sincerity. It is a good idea to be flexible, but it is also sensible to have some notion of what you would like to do. One of the most effective workers today in a well-baby clinic in Chicago is a former kindergarten teacher. But before she found her present happy post she wandered hither and yon, first trying to do for nothing what she had formerly been paid for, and then trying to enroll as a Gray Lady in a hospital that had rigid age limitations. Finally, through the American National Red Cross, she found her real métier. For the past decade she has been a devoted receptionist and registrar. Her warmth charms both mothers and children, and her careful record-keeping enables nurses and aides in the well-baby clinic to go about their own business with easy minds.

If all you have ever done to relax is to play bridge, will that be helpful? Certainly! Young people's groups, adult clubs, day-centers, nursing homes—there are many places to use that skill.

Are you a golfer or a tennis player or a baseball fan? What about the Boy or Girl Scouts? Or a prison's recreation ground? Or the nearest camp for disadvantaged boys and girls?

Ask Yourself Candid Questions

When you have assayed your talents verbally or otherwise, do not stop there. Certain questions ought to be faced and answered with candor; anticipate the queries you are going to have, and in an interview offer frank answers. The key word is honesty, with yourself as well as with your interviewer.

How much time are you able to give on a consistent basis to whatever you agree to undertake? The important word is "consistent." If you are able to come only once in awhile, say so; others do. There are always routine jobs to be done, and they will not be beneath your intelligence or experience if you realize they are necessary. But people who drop out after a few halfhearted visits give agencies pause and make it hard for their successors.

Are your vacations longer and do they come oftener than they used to? Do you travel more frequently and for greater periods of time? Are your goings and comings from town on a regular basis or erratic?

No one will begrudge your added leisure or the leave of absence you may want occasionally, provided you are honest about disclosing the need—in advance. If you have to be replaced at short notice—or none at all, you work a hardship on other people, both on the paid and on the volunteer staff. As a consequence, if you are thought to be unreliable, you may be reduced to a bottom-of-the-ladder assignment when you return. The real point at issue, however, is your acceptance of the responsibility for lifting a burden, not adding to the troubles an organization already has.

Frankness is all that is required. If you cannot do heavy lifting, much stooping, long standing, or read for hours without strain, say so—but at the same time add what you can do well and with ease. There is nothing disagreeable about admitting that the spirit is willing but the body has to be catered to, because it need not be an impossible barrier to what you want to do. Thousands of totally deaf, totally blind or other people suffering from grim handicaps, are among the most faithful and understanding in their efforts to alleviate other people's ills. A typical example is the woman who has not been able to leave her tiny one-room apartment for more than a decade; there she is confined to a wheelchair. She has a very small income, coupled with a great love of everything in nature. She gratifies it by raising miniature plants on her two windowsills. As they flower, she supplies dwarf geraniums to the wards in the hospital for orthopedic diseases where she was a patient for many months.

In your own self-appraisal take into account not only possible physical frailties but daily expenses. If spending money for lunch and transportation is a minor problem, do not hesitate to say so. Some agencies reimburse such costs as transportation. Others offer lunchroom facilities free. This is in no sense to be regarded as a charity. It is an investment in people generous with their time, strength, and talent, doing a job the organization regards as useful.

There are a few large institutions in outlying areas of great cities which sometimes arrange to pick up volunteers at a central spot and convey them to work and back again via bus. This practice is not general. Therefore, if you cannot drive your own car, or find a place in a car pool, and public transportation is not convenient, the obvious answer is not to expect a director of volunteers to solve your problem no matter how much you would like to work under his or her direction. There are always other avenues to explore. One pastor keeps this reminder conspicuously posted on a bulletin board:

You don't have to be a physician to be a healer.
You don't have to be a nurse to aid the ill and the lonely.
You don't have to be a man of the cloth or wear a nun's habit to hold out a helping hand in a moment of crisis.
You don't even have to be a parent to pass along your experiences to boys and girls in camps or schools.
You don't have to wait for the day when you'll have nothing but leisure; to have something to do, help someone else along the road you've already traveled; the time to begin is *now*.

It is said the "Over-60" club in his church has given more hours of free service to community-wide organizations than any other group with the same number of members, of any age, in the city.

Working Independently

Most types of volunteering involve interrelationships. But if you are the kind of person who works best on an independent basis, you can do that, too. Every metropolis suffers from depersonalization and lacks some services; if you can supply one or the other you will not need to do more than let the fact be known.

There is a distinguished Pennsylvania lawyer, for example, now in his vigorous eighties, who has never ceased to maintain his extensive offices and staff. But for the past dozen years or so he has accepted as clients only those who cannot pay regular legal fees; his rate is $1.00 for each visit. His waiting rooms are always full of men and women referred to him by his fellows in the Bar Association.

You may even want to try to rouse others about a cause about which you feel strongly. A New England physician with a lucrative practice surprised everybody but his wife when he announced he was retiring. He moved to the Deep South where the couple established a medical clinic where there was none before. His efforts on behalf of a wretchedly poor clientele, plus that of his wife (who before her marriage was a registered nurse), are supplemented by Northern colleagues. They volunteer their own services on a summer or winter vacation.

There is literally no human frailty that has not been overcome by those who share the philosophy of the late Dr. Albert Schweitzer. Once when he was addressing a boys' school he said, "I know one thing—the only ones among you who will be really happy are those who have sought and found how to serve."

It is human, however, to excuse oneself for not attempting to right the wrongs of the world we rail against, but if you think you have a viable reason to withdraw from the fight, consider the consistent record of a woman like Mrs. Lucy M. Ellis.

Mrs. Ellis is a childless widow, no longer young. For years she has been both homebound and bedbound; her limbs are paralyzed. But during those years, with only the use of one hand and a telephone and the warmth of her personality, she has accomplished her aim in Wethersfield, Connecticut. She has made "folks forget I'm handicapped; people had to be educated to ask a person like me to help."

That help has extended far beyond her own community in two decades of service marked by her vast interest in people. She has served as chairman or co-chairman of community drives ranging from the Community Chest to polio campaigns. She helped found a

Friends of the Library Association, aided the American Legion, runs the Girl Scout uniform exchange, plans Boy Scout programs, meets with den mothers, carries on follow-up work for the Businessman's and Civic Associations—and a host of other activities.

Since her husband's death Mrs. Ellis has lived alone and manages to keep her home going with only part-time household and nursing help. At the end of more than a quarter-century of civic service she could say, "Life has been good to me, and I'm so glad I'm needed in this world!"

The Art of Friendly Visiting

If you prefer to work in close contact with individuals, and perhaps actually see the fruits of what you do, what is aptly termed "friendly visiting" may be what you would like best. In any case, since it plays such a large part in programs in a multitude of many kinds of organizations, you ought to understand its function in your own community.

First of all, the prototype of ladies' bountiful—or that of their husbands—who had a few hours to spare and a few basketfuls of goodies to distribute before a feastday or a national holiday is no longer acceptable anywhere—if it ever was.

"Friendly visiting" as it is used today, requires some training in how to pay a visit. For it is one thing to call on a neighbor or friend or an acquaintance with whom you have something in common, and quite another to call on a sick child or a despondent stranger in a hospital or nursing home or some other institution.

Organizations recruit both individuals and whole groups; the latter may be part of some club or multi-purpose center or a lodge and prefer to do their visiting together and in one place. Lonely people waiting for the door to open represent many kinds and types of persons: disabled children, hospitalized citizens or veterans, those confined to institutions, or solitary adults unable to do their marketing or to go to church or to the doctor unaccompanied—the whole gamut of society, and not always those in the low income brackets.

The U.S. Public Health Service in one of its reports estimated that there are at least a million persons permanently confined to their homes, and another three and a half million partially or temporarily limited in their ability to quit their domiciles. The need to make their lives less desolate is very great.

The National Easter Seal Society for Crippled Children and Adults, which carries on its work in every state of the union, spells out the opportunities in these words:

> The Friendly Visitor . . . provides the socialization and an opportunity for participation in leisure activities. The Visitor is a sympathetic listener, a friend who remembers holidays and birthdays, a helper on trips out of the home. He may bring quiet games for the restless child, arts or crafts for the listless or bored; he may write a letter for the person who has poor use of hands, run an errand, or read to the elderly. . . . For many of these, the Friendly Visitor may become the vital link to the outside world.

Most organizations that sponsor such programs have short training courses; after that you will not be working entirely alone, but under the supervision of a staff member who is usually a social worker or a therapist.

The Easter Seal Society's own Home Service program grew out of the idea of one young mother when she became aware of shut-in children's needs through her small son's long-time illness. If your own city does not have a service similar to that which began in New York City over two decades ago, you yourself can start one, as Mrs. Margery McMullin did. She spent two years as a volunteer in a children's hospital, and then with no more help than that of concerned local university students, she started what has been called "the most unusual organization in New York." Its sole purpose is to bring fun, learning, companionship, and a bit of the outside world to boys and girls cut off from ordinary opportunities all children ought to have the right to enjoy. What is accomplished through the sensitive understanding that volunteers, young and old, give on regular weekly visits, is summed up in this story. It tells what one woman's visits mean to a twelve-year-old victim of muscular dystrophy:

> He sits in a wheel chair as he has for the last six years; it is equipped with a writing board and placed close to the specially built case in which he keeps his books, games, drawings, stamp and coin collections. His

59

visitor comes once every seven days; she has been doing it for six years. She is a year-round Santa Claus who through her personality, warmth and affection brings Billy his only contacts with the world outside.

Such a service can be started anywhere, at any age. For further information, write

>Director, Home Service
>Easter Seal Society for
>   Crippled Children and Adults
>239 Park Avenue, South, New York, N.Y. 10003

After You Are Accepted

The basic training sessions given in most large organizations to new volunteers are usually brief and not onerous. After that, you will be expected to adapt yourself to whatever rules and regulations the agency has. If you work with people who, in the current usage of our time, are "disadvantaged"—the poor, the sick, the institutionalized—it is assumed you will know that to be effective you must show respect for human dignity, privacy, and independence in exactly the same measure as you expect those privileges for yourself. It is also assumed you will be friendly and receptive, as well as responsive, without being effusive or patronizing. If you work with older people, you will need to recall that aging is not necessarily a synonym for senility; and at the other end of the life scale you must also realize that even the very young dislike to be overwhelmed with solicitude, however well meant.

Large organizations in the nonprofit fields usually have a special staff person assigned to be a director of volunteers, who is there to smooth the way. Where there is no such director, come as a beginner should, asking as few questions as you can, observing much, doing what you are given to do. Do not expect favors either because of your past work or past prestige or because of your white hairs, if any. (It has been said, not altogether jokingly, that to work with volunteers requires the patience of Job, the wisdom of Solomon, and the hide of a rhinocerous.)

In most cases you will be introduced to fellow volunteers and to the staff members by the head of the department you will work in. It is her privilege and duty to make it clear you are there as a welcome addition, to supplement, not supplant the paid staff. You will have to keep in mind always that you are a member of a team and that the paid employees on it consider they have been selected for their ability to do the job they are paid to execute. If you encounter on the part of the young or the uninformed any reluctance to explain duties to you, a beginner, this is a common malaise and has little to do with the fact of pay or non-pay. Be patient; if you find you cannot get the hang of what you are supposed to be doing, go to the head and discuss it frankly. Coldness will certainly not exist on the top level, toward volunteers, or you would not be there at all. Heads of organizations fully realize that a good volunteer can enrich the program of an agency by contributing talents, bring a sense of enthusiasm and dedication, and most of all, balance the professionalism of a staff by representing the attitudes of lay people in the community, thereby keeping the organization from becoming too detached.

What You Can Expect

What have you a right to expect in return for your goodwill, your honest desire to help? Much depends on your knowledge and acceptance of the fact that every person who donates part or all of a day, or a week, is useful in exact proportion to the time and effort, not that *he* puts in, but that he saves others equipped professionally to do what he cannot. This is a rule-of-thumb too often dishonored because many volunteers expect too much. One YMCA director puts it in these vigorous words: "This is the type who comes in the front door to offer his services forthwith as chairman of the board, or at the least, chairman of a committee." The fact that the person may have actually been chairman of a board of directors does not qualify him or her for a similar post of responsibility in an organization that may have entirely different aims which he has no training to interpret either to the staff or to the public.

The head of this enormous YMCA solved his own problems by drawing up a neat mimeographed list headed "Jobs that need to be done in this institution for which we cannot pay." Each potential helper, filled with the laudatory aim of being useful, is courteously received by an amiable receptionist and seated at a desk with the list before him. He is invited to make check marks at the places and jobs he thinks his background fits him for. It is a chastening experience, but one that has borne good fruit. The volunteer list at that YMCA is long and illustrious, and the men and women on it serve with distinction.

What someone has dubbed "a volunteer's bill of rights" is summed up in this guise:

1. You have a right to ask for a suitable assignment and to expect consideration to be given your preferences, your temperament, your education, and your experience.

2. You have a right to be given information in advance, about the organization you are joining, its policies, its programs, and its objectives.

3. You have a right to know where and when you will work and be assigned in an orderly way to some place that fits the job you will be doing.

4. You have a right to expect to have an orientation session, and if necessary, a training period.

5. You have the right to guidance and direction by some person assigned to invest time in giving it.

6. You have the right to expect to engage in a variety of experiences if you are able to execute them when they arise.

7. You have the right to know about any new developments in the organization which may give you a chance to expand your services.

8. You have a right to continuing education if you prove worthy of it, for greater responsibilities.

9. You have the right to be heard by some person in authority if you have queries or complaints.

10. You have a right to be treated as a bona fide co-worker of the regular staff, regardless of the fact that you are not receiving a salary.

The Rewards

What are the rewards in the channels you may seek? They will chiefly be the intangibles—the consciousness of a job well done, the good feeling that comes when one realizes he is not yet all "used up" no matter what his chronological age may be, the exhilaration of realizing that age brings with it knowledge and the experience to use it. All these are the essential ingredients in the recipe for happiness in any job. Occasionally a grateful community will single out some for special public praise; when it comes it is sweet, but do not look for it.

A few places may follow the example set by Chicago. Each year in May, during national observance of "Senior Citizens' Month," Chicago makes known the current honor roll in its "Hall of Fame." Older men and women are nominated for it by organizations to which they have made "significant and continuing contributions." In the now long annual list there are people like Marie Bell. She is a retired social worker who learned to lip-read at the age of seventy-eight. Two years later she was teaching regularly at the Chicago Hearing Society. The year she won a richly deserved place in the Hall of Fame, Carl G. Weiss did the same. He was a retired tool-room machine specialist who at seventy was operating an amateur radio station for patients in a veterans' hospital. And there was also Mrs. Ella B. Bohannon, aged ninety, who had received her bachelor's degree at the age of sixty-two. After that she devoted her time and years to helping young and old students seek educational achievements like her own.

As the citation on Chicago's long Honor Roll points out, "The example of their efforts and dedication to the civilizing process is worthy of emulation by all men regardless of age."

This sort of recognition is rare, and for most people it is not necessary. If you feel yourself part of any movement, you are bound to know that you have a part in whatever success is achieved, whether your share is large or small.

63

The Final Rewards

Good volunteers are *made,* not born. There may come a time when your initial enthusiasm, your motivation, or your energies begin to flag. You may even have become a little skeptical about the choice of agency you have made or its value to the community in proportion to its financial support.

This attitude usually means one of two things. Either you have made a wrong choice so far as you, yourself, are concerned, or your honeymoon stage is over, and you have to look at what is being done in the light of practical possibilities of realization.

If you were frank in your preliminary interviews, and the interviewer equally so with you, there is less likelihood that you will ever go through this phase of having to whip up your interest. But if the time does come when the first glow of enthusiasm you began with seems to be fading out, realize that the fault may not be in the agency or its probably harried staff, but in yourself. It is necessary to realize that the bulk of work done in this world, whether voluntary or paid for in cash, has to be executed on a steady, day-by-day basis and that the few highlights that brighten the way do not come at regular intervals, like traffic lights. If you continue to feel a drop in enthusiasm and self-questioning does arise, it is time to ask yourself whether you are really working to serve your fellowman or chiefly yourself.

Granted that it is a Herculean task for any organization to revive the spirit of neighborliness that existed of necessity in America's pioneer days. Nevertheless, you must keep before you always that this is the major objective in enlisting support and action on the part of the unpaid public.

Do you have any assurance you will have personal satisfaction? If you really believe in the cause, it would certainly seem so, as this one small story fully illustrates.

A large Massachusetts hospital reported on its tenth anniversary that of ninety-four volunteers who had registered for its first orientation course a decade before, fifty-seven were still active. Their ten years of service totaled almost 71,000 hours. What they did ranged from rolling surgical bandages a few hours once a week to conducting daily tours of visitors through laboratories and teaching facilities.

Every one of these "old faithfuls" in that group of fifty-seven had passed his or her sixty-fifth birthday before donating their first hour.

You can find thousands of people like this in any great city, and they are not do-gooders with a few idle hours to fill. Very often they are unseen and unheard, quietly doing some unspectacular task simply because it needs to be done, not asking or expecting public attention or acclaim. Many times they are not known by the ultimate beneficiaries of their work. Occasionally reward will be paid in the form of a tribute made at a public gathering; much more often it will come in the quiet satisfaction they experience in knowing they have done something to contribute to the betterment of the society in which they live, or for the one that will come after them. Sometimes their lives are enriched by the knowledge that they have been able to help just one individual. That is reward enough.

Chapter IV

Central Sources
For Urban Information

Most of us would like to say, as Dr. Arthur E. Morgan did long after he retired from the presidency of Antioch College, "I am not an individual but an element in human society in what I can do that is of value." But the majority of us who have lived long enough to realize this have to seek agencies through which we can use our capabilities. Yet, trudging from one to another to find the one that can best utilize your talents can be a time-consuming, even a nerve-wracking job. If you do it, you may have to be interviewed more than once, even in the same organization. Furthermore, going from door to door to find something that pleases you—and that you may please—often means a use of costly professional time to keep a round peg from trying to fit itself into a square hole. Or, to put it more charitably, it takes a skilled person to uncover and assay the talents even of the person eager and willing to help promote a good cause.

The Volunteer Service Bureau

You will save time and perhaps avoid disappointment, and organizations themselves will benefit, if you use one of the shortcuts

66

to information about volunteering open to you in any urban setting. This is true even if you think you know the exact agency through which you want to work. Change is in the air in our time, and something you were familiar with and upheld in earlier years may have gone through a metamorphosis you are not familiar with or may not even want to support.

The easiest way, therefore, to match what you want to give to provide the most satisfaction for yourself and offer your community its greatest return, is to use one of several types of central bureaus that act as clearinghouses for nonprofit agencies in need of volunteer help. The most common is one of the approximately one hundred and fifty in the United States which carry the name "Volunteer Service Bureau" or some variation of it. Their primary concern is to act as consultants to agencies on all matters of citizen participation. They recruit and refer men and women to match specific needs with available talents, for health, welfare, recreation, and cultural organizations.

The first such bureau was organized in Boston in 1926; during the last forty years they have become an integral part of the community planning process in most of the major cities of this country and Canada. Volunteer service bureaus function under the umbrella of the central fund-raising agency, but since the name of the latter varies from place to place, look for it under one or another of these in your telephone book: United Way, Community Chest, United Funds, Health and Welfare Council, United Appeal, Council of Social Agencies, Community Service Council, and so on.

Although all bureaus function independently, most of them belong to the Association of Volunteer Bureaus of America. If you have any difficulty locating the one in your area, or if you are moving to a new community and want to become active there, address a query to

Association of Volunteer Bureaus of America
c/o United Community Funds and Councils of America
345 East 46th Street, New York, N.Y. 10017

All local bureaus act as a bridge to bring together the needs of the individual and the needs of his community in an efficient manner. Wherever you live you will find that its policies are set by leaders from all areas of community life. In one Michigan city, for instance, the Advisory Committee consisted of representatives from business, education, health, law, labor, and social work agencies. Affiliated organizations respect this type of central pool because they know the volunteer who comes from it will be carefully selected and therefore will be a capable auxiliary. While an agency usually reserves the right to make a final decision about accepting (or rejecting) a volunteer there is little reason to fear such a veto because every attempt is made to match the person to the job. Your age will not matter one whit; your capabilities will.

The Advantages of Central Placement

The advantages in going to such a bureau are several. In the first place, this is one more weapon in the battle to keep under control the impersonality that cities breed. A voluntary service bureau has the names, addresses, and programs of all the agencies you are likely to be interested in and what their current needs for volunteers are. You will be interviewed by a capable person, usually someone who has been trained in the fields of education, social work, personnel, or psychology. She will know how to talk to and be talked to by people of all ages and walks of life. Because her job involves meeting many kinds of people she will be able to put you at your ease.

Appointments for an interview ought to be made, if possible, in advance. When you arrive you can ask frank questions and expect to receive candid replies. During what may seem to you to be a free-flowing conversation, the interviewer will be skillfully eliciting information about you to find out where you can be used to the best advantage.

In short, the interview is designed to evaluate you along the following lines:

1. *Ability to communicate.* (This involves vocabulary, rapport, loquaciousness, relevance, speech.)

2. *Appearance* (No one will question your fashion, but, obviously, you are expected to be neatly dressed, and give what the specialists call "a good adult image.")

3. *Initiative* (This word is all-embracing; the trained eye and ear are supposed to be able to judge your degree of aggressiveness, imagination, creativity.)

4. *Objectivity* (A word that covers self-discipline or its contrary, a tendency to over-forcefulness or evidence of bias.)

The interview itself will not be formidable. Naturally you will be asked about your education, work experience if any, past record of volunteering, and present preferences. Whatever you say will be held in confidence. While you ask or answer queries, the interviewer will be discreetly taking into account your general attitude, your probable dependability, your personality, and of course, special assets.

In going through a central bureau like this you avoid the embarrassment of commitment to something you may not like after you have plunged into it with too little knowledge, and which may not like you. This can happen if you take a post in an organization that suffers from too flamboyant publicity—and sometimes when it has not. On the other hand, at a volunteer service bureau, the over-eager person who has ignored Socrates' dictum, "Know thyself!" is tactfully re-routed where he ought to go. Here are two examples of such acumen:

In a large Midwestern city a man, recently retired, advised his interviewer he would like to teach certain crafts in which he was highly skilled because they had been a long-time hobby. Unfortunately he was almost deaf; the bureau considered his idea impractical. However, Mr. X. had behind him many years of experience as an editor. He eventually accepted a post in a center on alcoholism with whose aims he was found to be in great sympathy. There he reads and edits for publication summaries of newly published materials for use by the professional staff and does it with great despatch and enthusiasm.

In another city a woman applied for an occupational therapy assignment in a veterans' hospital. But in the course of the interview she disclosed the fact that she really preferred to work with children but had no pedagogical training for small fry. She was delighted to learn she could enter a course to learn how to teach homebound boys and girls. The head of the department in the agency in which Mrs. X. now works calls her "our jewel."

Any volunteer needs this kind of skilled help, but if you have had long experience behind you, you need it even more because you have to guard yourself against a tendency to want to teach rather than learn. But a central bureau will not make the mistake of putting you into a "class." The general attitude you will encounter is well expressed by Mrs. Anne Nicholson, the Director of the Volunteer Service Bureau of Minneapolis.

"To us," she says, "the so-called senior citizens are people like any other age group, with their individual likes and dislikes, skills, interests, backgrounds, personalities, and so forth. Their age is purely incidental."

Actually, you will find that there will be many volunteers in your own age bracket, no matter what it is, because there is a much greater interest in remaining part of the mainstream of life among the "so-called senior citizens" than there was even a decade ago. A recent report from the Council on Volunteers of Philadelphia is typical of many. About one-third of the men and women interviewed for city-wide agencies came from the retired group, aged sixty-five years and over. The report says, "They are referred after a determination of their ability to offer the kind of skills in jobs where they can fit."

This attitude is typical, and so is the age group. In Minneapolis, one-third of all adults who registered during an average twelve-month period at the Volunteer Service Bureau were over sixty years old, although the over-sixty age group represents only about 13 percent of the total population in the city. The age range was from sixty-two to eighty-five. But even this is less significant than the fact that two-thirds of them had served either as "regular" volunteers or were "on call" for a period ranging from four to fifteen years.

Being on call—which is another term for "spot volunteering"—may suit you better than working with just one agency and ordinarily gives you more latitude in disposal of your time, though you are not expected to take your work more lightly. Although you will not be tied down to just one place or one agency, usually you will be working at the same kind of tasks with different co-workers. Usually

70

the work requires no special techniques or training. Here is a sampling from the Minneapolis group which tells you it gives variety enough to some people:

Mr. A. at seventy-five works every day he can; in 1967 he gave 2,122 hours. His occupation is listed in the city directory as "assembler." His employer is the Volunteer Service Bureau itself.

Mr. B. is seventy-seven. The day after he retired he came to the Bureau and offered to help. He had been an auditor and he said he wanted "any job just so it isn't accounting!" During the next four months he put in 257 hours in simple clerical work and declared he enjoyed it.

The "regulars" also represent a cross-section of mankind, and you are likely to encounter their like anywhere.

Miss M. is eighty-seven. She is a former librarian with two college degrees. She stuffs envelopes for World Pen Pals. The job is not boring to her because she is interested in its ultimate aim. She also says she enjoys the company she meets where she works.

Miss S. is only sixty-six; she has a Ph.D. in physics. She calls herself a "rock hound" and teaches lapidary work in a multiple-purpose center for the elderly.

Mr. F. is still younger; he is sixty-four, a former bookkeeper. For fifteen years he led a chorus at his place of business. He volunteers one day at a hospital. Another day he leads group singing at a home for the aged for Norwegians. He says, "It's such fun to sing Norwegian songs, I jumped at the chance!"

The same variety of jobs exists in smaller cities, and the same stress will be laid on channeling your time and talents into areas where they can reinforce the professional staff. In Flint, Michigan, for instance, the Volunteer Service Bureau from time to time inserts "advertisements" in issues of a magazine that is locally circulated to the older population. This is representative of the list of opportunities in one issue, and not dissimilar to those you can find practically everywhere:

Clinic hostess: Wanted, someone to greet parents, help with wraps, weigh and measure infants and small children, and work at creating a comfortable and pleasant atmosphere for patients. (One day a week.)

Pianist needed: To play simple children's songs and nursery tunes for pre-school handicapped children. (9:00 to 9:30 A.M. one morning per week.)

Tour leader wanted: To assist agency staff in conducting tours of facilities for guests from USA and abroad. Agency may train volunteer to conduct tours. (Several times each month).

Tutor desired: to work with one child, talking, interpreting school assignments, as part of child's therapy. Needed at study hour period during school year. (6:30 to 7:30 P.M. or 7:30 to 8:30 P.M. weekdays only.)

And so on, through the gamut of human experience.

In California a volunteer service bureau was created specially to recruit older men and women. It gained such momentum that it gradually emerged as a community force that was recruiting volunteers of all ages for nearly a hundred nonprofit agencies. In one of its reports these significant statements were made:

"While placements are made for people in all income brackets, the volunteer giving the largest number of hours last year was a recipient of old age assistance. . . . Despite removal of its age limitation and enthusiastic participation by youngsters, particularly in summer months, nearly half of the volunteer hours are contributed by the nucleus of senior volunteers."

If you want a good account of the service rendered, send for

A Project Study on Volunteer Work
Administration on Aging
Washington, D.C. 20201
AOA publication No. 902, April, 1967 (free)

Utilizing Chambers of Commerce

One other central source of information more widespread than the volunteer service bureaus but too often disregarded by retirees, are local chambers of commerce. Since they flourish in both large cities and small and number nearly five thousand, they are accessible to nearly everybody, sometimes even in villages.

Too often chambers of commerce—sometimes known as boards of trade—are thought of as civic organizations whose sole purpose is to serve industry and to try to evolve methods of attracting new businesses. Their other functions deserve to be better known. Since they are set up to serve all citizens—not merely those in business—you are legitimately entitled to avail yourself of their services.

Chambers of commerce have been serving as central sources of information about everything that affects a citizen's life at any stage since 1848. In that year, in Cleveland, Ohio, the pattern was set. When the chamber of commerce was organized there its functions were to include not only industrial activities, but members were directed also "to take an active interest in housing, playgrounds, and good city government."

That early interest has been continued and expanded throughout the country. All chambers of commerce today take full account of the diverse ills that beset their communities, and are committed to doing something about them. Their doors are always open not only to respond to queries, but to offer a chance to those who want to help.

While structure, methods, and activities do differ from place to place, according to the size of the community and its problems and assets, all chambers follow a road sufficiently uniform to be defined by the national organization, the United States Chamber of Commerce in Washington, D.C., in these words: "A chamber of commerce is people working together to make their community a better place in which to live."

In the offices of a local chamber of commerce community needs are known and evaluated, and measures taken to improve public health, raise standards in civic work, develop better recreation facilities, and cultivate better understanding between diverse segments of the population.

Because of this widespread concern about everything that will benefit the inhabitants (not only its business concerns), whether you are an old resident or a newcomer, a personal call at the offices is a

73

good way to find out about your own community. If you are planning on moving to a new area, write the secretary-manager of the local chamber of commerce. You will find the following publication in most general public libraries, giving you names, addresses, and other information:

World Wide Chamber of Commerce Directory
Johnson Publishing Company, Inc.
Box 455
Loveland, Colorado 80537 ($3.00)

Every chamber carries on its activities through committees created to function in areas determined by a particular community's needs. If you are interested in civic problems and want to help solve them, the staff will tell you how it can make direct use of your services. Usually you will be invited to attend a meeting of the volunteers functioning on committees dealing with air pollution, zoning problems, schools, recreational areas, and so forth. If you seem to its members to have potentialities as a member, sooner or later you will be asked if you would like to join.

If you become active you will find yourself in congenial company. Committees are made up of the whole range of business and professional men and women—advertisers, bankers, clergymen, lawyers, manufacturers, physicians, retailers, salesmen, teachers, wholesalers. Everyone is a participant because he shares with his fellows a common interest and pride in the hometown, not only for what it is, but for what it can, or ought to be.

The number and enthusiasm of its own workers and how they perform their duties for the community as a whole is the way a chamber's board measures its effectiveness. Here are typical examples taken from the records of a chamber of commerce located in a California community that attracts many retired people. It is illustrative of the way in which you, too, may find sound outlets.

1. A retired merchant called on the Retail Committee and offered his services. He now assists the chairman in digging up promotional ideas. He also makes calls on local stores to help them coordinate

their selling activities. He is considered a major acquisition to the community.

2. An erstwhile engineer was told the Career Counselling panel could use him. His colleagues were delighted to find a man who could speak the language of county and state engineers. Now he is also engaged, as a member of another committee, trying to get better roads and better sewage disposal in his new hometown.

3. A woman dropped in one day and said she had nothing behind her but a department store career. She was persuaded she could sell memberships to the Chamber as well as she used to sell lingerie. She finds her new job exhilarating and the contacts stimulating.

Inquire at City Hall

While there is no direct connection between chambers of commerce and efforts launched through the mayor's office in a number of cities trying to fight human and structural blight, there is a bridge between the two, and frequently the work men and women are doing to cope with urban malaise is intermeshed.

There are jobs that urgently need your and everybody's help because the paid employees on a municipal staff cannot cope with all the urgent civic problems that exist. The help of citizens from all ranks of society—regardless of age—is needed. In New York City a Volunteer Coordinating Council was formed in 1966—the first in the country—whose purpose is to induce more men and women to serve as volunteers in undermanned municipal departments. In its first year of operation ten thousand requests were made by heads of New York's bureaus and departments for part-time and occasional help.

Other cities have New York's problems and need the same kind of citizen aid, whether they have a special committee formed for the purpose of recruiting it or not. A Mayor's Advisory Committee on Services to the Aging was launched in Philadelphia, and Baltimore has its own effective version. Chicago was the first city in the United States to have a Commission expressly established to study older people's needs and how to meet them; a decade or so later the Commission was formerly made a legal part of the municipal government.

But you do not need to confine yourself to offering help only to benefit the aging. Any city hall, anywhere, welcomes participation by the public, and you do not have to be a politician to merit attention.

The following are random samplings of what conscientious older citizens in all parts of the country found to do when they offered to put their shoulder to the creaking municipal wheels:

1. In a Midwestern city a newspaper story mobilized hundreds of men and women past their sixtieth birthday who volunteered to work on a study dealing with the effects of current and proposed public transit costs on the mobility of the city's population.

2. In the Eastern part of the country older people rang doorbells to help take a census of the age categories of the local population. The primary purpose was to establish an accurate count of men and women over sixty-five, and to ascertain their interest or the contrary in proposed recreational centers.

3. On the West coast a city that attracts many retirees boasts that the boards of its police department, fire department, and two museums are chiefly directed by men and women past sixty. In the same area, city-owned beaches enroll retirees as voluntary lifeguards, swimming instructors, teachers of first aid, and playground directors.

A telephone ring or a letter to your own mayor's office should be enough to get started. For, as one councilman said, "There is a perennial crisis in government, and what's needed is more men and women to cure or prevent it, working quietly and methodically behind the scenes."

You do not need to wait till some council or commission is started to enlist aid. The best workers are often the ones who simply see what needs to be done and do it. One old man in a Southern city that has suffered frequent river flooding puts in four hours a day each week serving on a county disaster council whose objective is prevention. Another who was once a city official himself, and is now homebound, finds it rewarding to do typing and clerical work for twelve different city agencies. He calls his telephone "my third arm." Mrs. O., now nearing seventy, still sews a fine seam. She no longer can go to the hospital where she used to be a ward assistant because her arthritis makes walking difficult. But she herself thought of the idea of making gay slip covers to brighten up the waiting room and children's nursery in this drab municipal institution. Mrs. O.'s finances are limited, and the department she used to work in buys her materials. But its head said, "We can't buy Mrs. O.'s kind of loving interest through the civil service's budget."

In short, a person moving into the second or third phase of his life can and should accommodate himself not only to changed times but to the changes in his own life. One way to do it is to move a little out of the beaten path of the philanthropic organizations to see what other vistas there are. The greater the problems in your area, the more interested people can alleviate if not cure them. You need not even be allied with a political party to assume a real role. City Hall is the place to offer your help. Its ultimate aim ought to be better government, but it cannot come about only through elected officials. It is a job for the citizenry.

The Multipurpose Center

Evidence that older men and women are being counted on more and more to function as positive forces for good for themselves, first of all, and for others, can be found in multipurpose centers. They sprang up originally as so-called day centers, but they are a far cry now from the first version. When the William Hodson Day Center opened its doors in 1943 in the Bronx, New York, its avowed purpose was to provide recreation and activities for lonely older people, chiefly those living on small incomes. Today, used by nearly twenty million older men and women representing all types and all kinds of Americans, multipurpose centers reach out in numerous directions to give men and women in the upper age brackets all kinds of opportunities to remain active.

The National Council on Aging, which acts as a clearing house to help find administrators, social workers, adult education teachers, and recreational instructors to man a constantly increasing number of centers, large and small, all over the country, defines them in these words: "A center is a place to which older people come to enjoy the companionship of their peers and to participate in programs of activities and services that are meaningful for the later years of life."

If you have never visited one, your first trip may be an eye-opener. There is the opportunity to secure individual counseling if you need it; information on a variety of subjects; often extensive courses; a diverse program of amusements; and many, many outlets for community service with your peers. You will find other people like yourself, and some of them will be acting as volunteers to assist a paid professional staff. In a city such centers are open the year around, at least five days a week, sometimes during both daytimes and evenings. They are community supported.

New centers are being formed, if not overnight, at least too frequently for any national directory to be kept absolutely up to date; but if you have difficulty in finding the one nearest you, any local organization whose clientele include the aging can furnish the address. Or you can write

> National Council on the Aging
> 315 Park Avenue, S.
> New York City 10010

Or practically any large public library will have the latest edition of

> *National Directory of Senior Centers*
> prepared by Administration on Aging
> Washington, D.C. 20402 (first edition
> was 1966; revised in 1968)

Centers, large and small, represent one more attempt to overcome the depersonalization of our society. The scope of activities varies, but is well illustrated in two totally diverse types, located on opposite sides of the United States.

When Bronx River Neighborhood Centers (which offers programs to age groups ranging from preschool children to the very old) applied for a grant to help carry on its work, its application to Washington stated that volunteers should be older men and women who would be used

> to provide companionship, to act as assistants in nursing homes, operate meal and transportation services for the elderly, form part of a telephone reassurance team to make sure nothing is wrong in a room or home occupied by a solitary individual, and in some cases to do home repair or maintenance service so that older men and women could continue to live in their own homes.

The volunteers mentioned in the application would be selected from those already participating in the wide range of cultural, athletic, educational and social programs that the Bronx River Neighborhood Centers offer.

"Self-help" here is more than a slogan; it is the focus of all programs planned and carried out by those who call themselves "senior citizens." Their work is supervised by a board of directors (itself composed of older men and women) and conducted by four committees. They work in this fashion:

Individual Services Committee: Members give information, conduct a referral service, a "drop-in" emergency service, and offer help to long-time chronically ill patients.

Visitation Committee: They are responsible for home visits, meals-on-wheels, telephone reassurance programs for the homebound or isolated, recreation programs, group visits to nursing homes or to the permanently homebound or institutionalized.

Legislative and Publicity Committee: Members have the important function of educating not only the older person himself but the whole community on the needs of the elderly (and this is in a section of the Bronx where approximately 27,000 persons past sixty-five live). They also serve as a voice for their neighbors in situations that require legislative or social action.

Evening and Weekend Program Committee: Eight older citizens provide a full-day, full-week recreation and education program. It includes such events as concerts, dinners, movies, trips, cultural projects, and dances.

The metamorphosis that is taking place nationally is well illustrated by the history of "Little House Senior Activity Center." When it opened in Menlo Park, California, in 1949, sponsored then as now by the organization called Peninsula Volunteers, Inc. there were only twelve charter members. Today it has many hundreds who are members, and the center is open seven days and six nights a week. Its building has had to be enlarged three times to contain a constantly expanding program of educational, cultural, recreational, and community activities. It is a full-fledged agency member of the Community Council of San Mateo County. Little House government is democratic. The Peninsula Volunteers Board cooperates with the Little House Council in planning and policy, and a joint committee has financial responsibility for the operation of the programs, directed by a professional staff aided by senior volunteers.

Little House was cited for excellence by the Administration on Aging in these words:

> It provides an ideal place and multiple opportunities for senior citizens to find companionship; to discover new or pursue former interests in education, recreation, and craft activities; and to contribute to the welfare of their community.

The list of community responsibilities accepted by the members is long but is similar to what, with local variations, you will find elsewhere. Instead, therefore, of seeking out another agency to contribute services to, you can find an outlet for your talents in working for the center itself.

For instance, at Little House many instructors are recruited from nearby universities and school systems, but their number is augmented by Little House members. For instance, an engineer shares his knowledge with a lapidary class; an expert weaver not only teaches her craft but made another substantial contribution when she wove all the draperies for a new addition to Little House.

Many of the community efforts in which members engage in California will be open to you elsewhere, if you consult a multipurpose center. At Little House they

make monthly visits to the Veterans Administration Day Center
make equipment and toys for handicapped children
prepare layettes for the San Mateo County Adoption Unit
work with the Friendly Visitors Service
participate in the Foster Grandparents program
arrange a "share party" to provide Christmas gifts for needy families
organize annual Easter egg hunts for handicapped children
work with retarded adolescents in a socialization program

and so on, if not *ad infinitum,* at least for the benefit of themselves and others; no one can call a person who is this active "retired from life."

Old Service in New Dress

One does not have to go to the comparatively new multipurpose centers to realize a healthy attitude is emerging which is permitting a willing older person to be a participant rather than an onlooker.

The National Federation of Settlements and Neighborhood Centers estimates that willing men and women give from 75,000 to 100,000 hours of service each week in more than 90 major cities of the United States. It is a safe guess that many of those hours were donated by people old enough to remember when the name of Jane Addams illuminated the field of social work. She founded the famous settlement, Hull House, in Chicago, and said not only of it but of every place and every time, "It is the good you do *with* people, not *for* people, *that* is most enduring."

It is this philosophy which governs the work of over four hundred settlements and neighborhood centers throughout the country. They continue to help people to act in joint ventures on their own behalf in the urban locality where they feel most at home, just as they did when the settlement idea was born in the United States with the establishment of the happily named "Neighborhood Guild" of New York City in 1886. Today's version has kept pace with the times. From city to city the program may vary but everywhere trained men and women, aided by volunteers differing in age and capabilities, are trying to find today's solutions for yesterday's problems.

It is only in the past century that social work has been professionalized. Before that it was done on a volunteer basis and still depends on millions of unpaid people willing to engage in a battle on behalf of the sick, the handicapped, and the socially deprived.

If you wonder what you can do, the answer is that if you call at the nearby settlement or neighborhood center, you will be given personal help in finding out. It may be that you will find your post at the settlement itself. One executive director, asked what kind of people she could use, ticked off on her fingers, alphabetically, "Artists, beauticians, businessmen, craftsmen, dentists, educators, fiddlers, geologists, housewives—and all the way to Z!"

Specifically, if you can give a day or two each week, or several hours daily or weekly, or even an entire winter or summer, you will be directed to vacancies in day care, child tutoring, adult education, community recreation, or home services, plus a wide range of social action efforts. They include everything from voter registration drives to helping rouse individuals' sense of responsibility so that they will work with their neighbors to remedy a specific evil where they live.

There may be a chance to work on a person-to-person basis, either with adults or with children. You may prefer to undertake administrative tasks, the kind that underlie every piece of welfare work, small or large. You may have the capacity to become an active committee member, or eventually serve on the board. Or you may just want to be the "grandparent" who helps out in a children's camp a week or two during the summer, or takes a group of boys and girls on a weekend or day-camping trip. You may be able to teach adults English, do census-taking, be involved in consumer education, or work on the community newspaper. From year to year, the scope varies, but the chance of boredom is negligible. Whatever you do will be geared to the changing needs of pepole in the city where you—and they— live.

Margaret E. Berry, the Executive Director of the National Federation of Settlements and Neighborhood Centers, spokesman for the 420 settlement centers in over 30 states, says this: "However late the hour there is time. . . . Settlements are one way for individuals and groups to get involved in positive action . . . in the neighborhood, the city, the region, and the nation."

The publications list contains leaflets of interest to laymen which define the scope of work on which you may someday want to engage. Among them are the following:

100,000 Hours a Week (Volunteers in Neighborhood Service to Youth and Families) November, 1964. $2.00.

The Volunteer and Community Welfare (What it means to be a local board member), by Frederick B. Taylor, October, 1965. $.30
Building Better Neighborhoods (History and Work of Settlements and Neighborhood Centers). May, 1966. $.07

Any central fund-raising agency in your city can furnish lists of settlements and neighborhood centers. Or you can write the national organization for information, plus a list of its publications and News about neighborhood developments anywhere in the country. Address

> Field Secretary
> National Federation of Settlements
> and Neighborhood Centers
> 232 Madison Avenue, New York City, N.Y. 10016

New Climates of Welcome in the Schools

One central source of volunteering which exists everywhere, and which has gone through an enormous transformation so far as attitudes toward older people are concerned, is the public school system. Only a few years ago schools that did not look askance at incorporating older men and women into their volunteer program were as rare as the dodo. Today some thousands of men and women of grandparent, and even great-grandparent age, are being welcomed in numerous capacities, and a great many are serving with distinction.

If you are concerned about how the young are being educated, and what kind of citizens they are likely to become, this is a major source of inquiry for you. The first program to use "grandparents" was the one that began in New York City with a pilot program in 1954.

Its chief objective was to help children overcome language and other barriers hindering their progress. It was so successful that subsequently the Ford Foundation sponsored twenty such projects for tutoring boys and girls on a one-to-one basis, or in small groups, in widely varying communities. The original projects were supervised through the National School program, an arm of the Public Education Association. Today several hundred communities have adapted the program with local variations. There are projects where only a few dozen volunteers are used, and there are cities where thousands, young and old, supplement what overworked professional staffs cannot do.

Boys and girls who benefit by this adjunct to the school program are not all poverty stricken, and not all foreign-born. They may come from families where a love of books and formal learning are lacking; or they may be at the other extreme, with quick minds and above average intelligence, restless because their minds do not have enough to feed on in the classroom.

Volunteering as valuable cogs in this new type of educational machine, men and women serve in these ways:

1. They give individual help, under professional supervision, to one child, or a small group. Where there is a foreign language barrier, aid in reading is important; it is not necessary to know the native language of the child, though it is an asset.

2. Volunteers' talents are used to enrich a classroom program, or one for the entire school, in such areas as art, music, photography, dramatics, geology, geography, gardening, and so forth.

3. So that teachers can do more teaching and less routine paper work, volunteers help with classroom study periods or in the library. They are also useful on playgrounds.

If you find out there is as yet no such formal school volunteering program in your community, you could still offer your services to a local school principal or to the school board. You might even prove to be the fomenting force to bring such a program into local being. (Guidelines in print have been laid down and educators know about them.)

If you have rapport with children—if you like them and get on well with them, whether or not their backgrounds are similar to yours—you can make a happy niche for yourself.

You need not hesitate for fear you will be too old to start. In New York City, at the age of eighty, Mrs. Kathleen Donay is still volunteering one very full day a week. She has to take two subway trains and a bus to get from her apartment to P.S. 129, and she has to leave her door at 8:00 A.M. But she makes it, even when the snow is deep.

Mrs. Donay is an ex-milliner whose lifetime hobby has been dressing dolls in historically accurate costumes. With this talent, plus her effervescent personality, Mrs. Donay was an instantaneous success. Under her direction, sewing groups began to make period costumes, using their handmade rag dolls as "models." Other sewing groups were taught by her to make all the costumes for the school's plays. But perhaps her greatest contribution has been made in a class of children who lost school time through serious illness or physical disabilities. She was able to catch their attention and hold their interest by teaching them history in her own unique, graphic way.

As Mrs. Donay's example shows, nobody need shy away from the idea of school volunteering for fear he has not the requisite professional background, or because his college days are far behind him, or nonexistent. Book learning and graduate degrees are useful, of course, but so are other talents. Your work, for instance, might consist of taking a traveling exhibit from a museum from school to school and talking about it, or demonstrating a craft at the school assembly. In Detroit members of Solidarity House, retired workers affiliated with the United Automobile Workers Union, have helped children in several elementary schools. They include an auto mechanic, a carpenter, a railroad worker, an accountant, housewives, hobby gardeners, amateur artists, and story-tellers. In Seattle, Washington, grandmothers acted as kindergarten aides, and a retired school cook was so attached to her charges she continued to serve them—but as a tutor four times a week.

If you wonder how school officials might react to nonprofessionals who have to be absorbed into their specialized areas, look at this excerpt from a tribute paid Howard Bede by the Board of Education in Winnetka, Illinois, a suburb of Chicago:

> Following his retirement as an executive in an advertising agency, Mr. Bede filled his life with volunteer activities in schools. He utilized his experience in his career, his skill in photography, his collection of rocks and unpolished stones, and most significantly, his unfaltering confidence in children as he works in the schools.

Mr. Bede was one of four retired businessmen recruited through the "Talent Pool" to work with one child or a small group of children forty minutes each week. That was in 1960. But several years later Mr. Bede was using different facets of the accumulated experience and hobbies of forty business years in seven schools; in addition he was working with sixty boys from underprivileged areas in Chicago during a summertime project. In 1968 Mr. Bede became the volunteer director of a unique seminar for school administrators, volunteer agencies, and community leaders for a "show-and-tell" conference. By that time Mr. Bede was also traveling to other Illinois communities where the idea of Winnetka's PAM (Project for Academic Motivation) had spread.

Mrs. Janet Freund, Director of the project, puts the mutual benefit to participants, and especially the retired person, in these cogent words: "The school volunteer projects not only offer an opportunity to get back into the 'game,' but the game itself is improved when the older adult volunteers along with others of goodwill to play it."

The Winnetka plan has now spread widely. These are a few of the things that retired men and women are doing:

1. A man with long experience in a telephone company worked on a communications experiment with junior-high-school boys.

2. An elderly woman who is a ceramics artist taught the beginnings of her craft to a second grade art class.

3. A former television weather reporter lectured on meteorology.

86

4. A geologist of international fame showed his collections of rocks and created interest in the collection of specimens and their identification among high-school boys.

5. A financier lectured to a seventh grade class in mathematics on banking procedures, and afterwards a former member of the stock exchange explained how it operates.

The Winnetka plan, which involves use of a trained coordinator responsible for matching teachers' requests and student needs with available volunteers, aroused such interest nationally that two publications have been prepared, adaptable anywhere. If your own community does not yet have school volunteers, or if it does and you think you would like to be one, make your request to the local Board of Education. (You might remember to say that from 25 percent to 33 percent of the PAM volunteers have always been in the over-sixty category, and 20 percent of the coordinators are at least sixty years of age.)

If there is no Talent Pool (which can be used for other types of recruiting besides school volunteers) and you want to work with others to form one, send for these two guides:

How to Set Up a Volunteer Talent Pool for Community Service. Write to PAM Project Director, 1155 Oak Street, Winnetka, Ill. 60098.

Operating Manual for a Volunteer Talent Pool. Compiled by Janet Burgoon and Joan Winter, 620 Lincoln Ave., Winnetka, Ill. 60093 ($2.25). *Note:* The Manual also contains material illustrating phases of the National School Volunteer Program.

And if you want to learn how school volunteering works in a metropolis where the men and women recruited as tutors *must* be at least forty years old, write for

Team in Action (T.E.A.M., Inc., standing for Talent, Experience, Ability, Maturity)
Community Chest Building
207 West Market St., Louisville, Ky. 40202

Change Along the Religious Front

For centuries past church and synagogue have been the one central source available to everybody for information, counsel, and personal aid. This is still true, with one major difference. This great community force is one in which the wind of change is blowing vigorously; in many instances this is resulting in long second looks, not only at the older members of a particular congregation, but at a program of social action that sometimes involves them.

Whether you are or are not a church-goer, if you live in a metropolis and want to find out what is happening there, probably the easiest method is to investigate what leading religious groups—Catholic, Protestant, and Jewish—are doing. In a large city it is likely that many of the large churches and synagogues will have staffs who can tell you not only what is going on within their own area but what other organizations are doing. You do not need to be a member to be received with courtesy and be given information, nor will you be pressed to join anything. The person who talks to you will have a professional (not a sanctimonious) attitude; he or she will be bearing witness to his faith in a manner corresponding and responding to fundamental changes going on throughout American society.

For churches and synagogues, on the whole, are showing a marked contrast to those complained of at the first White House Conference on Aging in 1961. At that time strong statements were made to the effect that religious groups were taking too few firm public stands on issues affecting the lives of millions of older people. Yet less than seven years later the picture had changed. At that time an official of the U.S. Administration on Aging, addressing a conference, said that at least one third of the Foster Grandparent programs launched by the Office of Economic Opportunity looked to churches either as their sole sponsoring agency or as their partial sponsors cooperating with a local institution in support of the program.

This effort, designed to give institutionalized children individual attention, is only one of the numerous efforts that are encouraging older men and women to maintain what one capable older pillar of her church calls "a cutting edge." Many denominations, taking cognizance of the fact that people are living increasingly longer, have a special staff, sometimes a whole department, charged with studying the concerns of the country's older population. This is not done with the limited idea of encouraging them to remain or to become church members, but by and large with the potent question of how to make their lives mean something to themselves and to others. This is not to say that the church or the synagogue everywhere is giving positive leadership on such vital issues nor are any religious groups monolithic bodies with control over each of their units. But if you are at loose ends and are exploring avenues for the future, you will find yourself cordially received if you drop in to see what a priest, rabbi, or minister, has to suggest. You may even find yourself talking to some volunteer, quite frequently an elderly one, who is capable of giving information or counsel. Do not fear that any pressure will be put on you to join this or that, or to participate in the life of a congregation if you have no desire to be a member. A great urban house of worship these days is an organization of many people fully aware of unrest in our society, and equally aware that it takes people of all kinds and all ages to help solve its problems.

If, on the other hand, you are or have been a church-going person, you will find that the traditional forms of voluntary work within the framework of the religious fold still exist. They can be yours in abundance if you make it known you have time and interest in doing them. Women still cook and serve luncheons and dinners, even in a great city; and people of both sexes see to it that the homebound are visited, transport the frail, or stage bazaars. There is still need for ushers and choir singers, and many people are needed to aid in the necessary business of seeing that buildings are kept in good repair or funds are raised for a new community house.

There are also growing in numbers a wide assortment of less orthodox ways to do your bit under the leadership of a religious institution. Members of Riverside Church's "Tower League" are an example. All participants must be over sixty years old. They help break down New York City's racial barriers by coaching students on a one-to-one basis, act in or direct drama or cinema groups, and participate in arranging affairs like the annual "Hispanic Festival." On church premises they are given the opportunity to roll surgical bandages or prepare Braille Christmas cards for local organizations for the blind. A large number of those who sign up for the programs are neither members of the church nor Protestants.

While this liberal attitude is not universal, it is becoming so. If you like the idea of offering home hospitality to foreigners, or coaching those who lack knowledge of English, or reaching out a helping hand in any other way, your own religious background will not be questioned if you want to put it to use under another banner.

At a summer conference on aging, held under the auspices of the American Baptists, nineteen ways were listed to show what older men and women could do within their local churches. Another seven were mentioned under the heading "wider church relationships." They comprised such civic activities as working within the YMCA or YWCA, or as interpreters with bilingual groups. A final listing of eight other avenues of community service was then made. It ranged from teaching in an adult literacy program to "being a friend" to a patient in a mental hospital or an institutionalized boy or girl.

If you are foot-loose and have a taste for far pastures for a summer, or a year or two, there is also ample opportunity to ally yourself with one or another church project that affects the lives of those disadvantaged by reason of poverty, sickness, color, or any other problem. Very often it is possible to become part of such worthwhile endeavors regardless of previous church affiliations, or if there have been none at all.

For instance, the Mobile Health Fairs, sponsored by the Board of National Missions of the Presbyterian Church, offer posts to qualified Protestants, Catholics, and Jews. The personnel who contribute their expert medical services are recruited on a nondenominational basis, without distinction as to race, color, creed, or age. These dedicated workers are physicians, dentists, nurses, and medical technicians who pay their own expenses to have the opportunity to give information that affects the lives of people in some of the most backward areas of our country. Very often one of these mobile summer fairs leaves behind it the beginnings of the first permanent health service a district in the Ozarks or a remote Allegheny area has ever known.

There are many other opportunities, sometimes more, and sometimes less spectacular, ranging from Indian reservations in the far

West to poverty stricken city ghettos in the East. If you have the right qualifications for a particular post, if you are hale and eager, you can operate a nursery school; supervise playground activities; act as a homemaker's consultant, a librarian, a thrift shop manager, an office secretary—or in a dozen other posts, usully on a short-time basis. The thing to do is to consult that useful central source of information, a religious institution. Or go to a library and look at the "want-ad" columns of denominational newspapers and magazines.

The General Outlook

This shift—sometimes swift, sometimes slow—in attitudes toward the usefulness latent in the long leisure years ahead of most of us, is not uniform and may never be. But it is already a proved fact within and without the government, that heads of organizations are learning that older people can be relied on, not only to want to help themselves if given a chance, but to help others. Many have already begun to realize that men and women in the upper age brackets who live alone or with a spouse, are capable of furnishing the same kind of love, patience, experience, and wisdom that used to be put to constructive use in a bygone era for the big family unit living under one roof. You may have to take the initiative; you may even have to prove you have something more than time to give. But if you really do want to remain a part of the stream of life, you should not hesitate to seek out—rather than wait to be sought by—those central sources of information that will help you find the right outlet.

Some wit has said that humanity is the only institution from which the old are not expected to retire.

Chapter V

Small Towns
and Rural Areas
Need You

Nowhere is your opportunity to do good for your fellowman more
vital, more urgent, than in what are sometimes mistakenly called
the idyllic rural regions.

For whether you are a regular summer visitor, or a year-round
resident, the poor will be all around you. Many of them will be your
own age, or older, for although the total rural population shows
a steady decline, the number of older people in proportion to it increases. In many instances they are the independent, proud, older
generation, nearly always left behind by their own choice when
young people leave in search of a more comfortable, easier town life.

If you have a lake cottage or a weekend or summer retreat in the
mountains, or even if you are a year-round resident in a village near
a city, are you sure you know enough about the life around the perim-
eter of the place you live? What kind of men and women are these,
your rural neighbors? In isolated areas, do the old-time virtues of
helping one's neighbor without recourse to outside aid still prevail?

In this day of rapid transportation and interdependence, when one county is no longer physically remote from another, is there any such thing as isolation?

The answers to these questions may startle you, especially if you find it difficult to penetrate the reserve habitual to many long-time residents in the country.

It is true there are wealthy Western ranchers, Southern plantation owners, and prosperous Northern dairy farmers. But the words "rural resident" also embrace the subsistence farmer in Appalachia, the Pennsylvania coal miner, the upstate New York villager, or even the factory worker who commutes to the nearest city to scratch out the living his acres no longer give him. In addition, there are the local physicians, lawyers, teachers, ministers, and merchants as well as the weekenders or the retirees who come in search of tranquility.

Your rural neighbors, that is, represent the same wide assortment as the rest of us, but some of their characteristics and many of their problems are unique.

If you really want to be part of the life around you, it is necessary to recognize that proportionately, there is more poverty in rural America than in our big cities. Those of us brought up on the romantic pictures that used to appear regularly around Thanksgiving time on magazine covers, showing grandma and grandpa puttering around the kitchen while they waited for their city children to gather around a harvest-filled table, may find it hard to believe this peaceful concept has altered. It is true that today grandpa mechanizes his farm as far as his finances permit, and grandma prepares her famous meals in a stainless steel kitchen like her city daughter has, when she can. But if you look under the surface of the apparently peaceful little villages and modest farms that still exist in some places, you will find unmet needs that are just as urgent as any in the squalor of a big city.

Poverty in Rural Areas

It is a shocking fact that in the United States today in what is the richest nation in history, close to 14,000,000 rural Americans are poor and a high proportion of them are destitute. . . . Some 30% of the total population live in rural areas but 40% of the nation's poor live there.

93

Contrary to popular impression all the rural poor do not live on farms
... most live in small towns and villages.

This is an excerpt from a report published in 1967 of the President's Committee on Rural Poverty. It is significantly titled "The People Left Behind."

Can you say, "We live in a rural area, too, and we don't have those problems"? Are you sure? What have you done to find out? It is no answer to point out that many forms of state and Federal assistance exist and they are the right of the disadvantaged in rural localities just as they are of city dwellers. Of course there are local and state-wide and Federal efforts to try to meet situations such as the report discloses, but poverty and isolation in the country are difficult to root out, and often there is lingering suspicion of officialdom.

Moreover, in contrast to a city, there are always fewer recreation facilities in proportion to the rural population, fewer public and private welfare agencies, fewer means of transportation, even fewer commercial facilities. No matter how much a small town may resemble a Currier & Ives picture, if you look beyond its simplicity you will find individuals or entire families living in sparsely populated areas, removed from whatever new developments there may be in housing or sanitation, often unable to take advantage even of medical facilities, great or small, or participate in any kind of social life. There *is* much national concern. There are home-aid services, visiting nurses, the help of the nationwide network of the Extension Service agents, the county welfare department, and many other attempts to help people in small towns and on farms to meet the challenges of that cliché we repeat when we talk of "our rapidly changing times." But there are never enough.

Furthermore, the bewildering adjustment to old age, which is often a personal crisis to millions of Americans elsewhere, is intensified in rural areas. Men and women who have been accustomed to hoe their own row all their lives—sometimes literally—may never have had a chance, or may never have wanted to participate in insurance or pension plans. With the breakdown of the old traditions of familial responsibility sometimes there is not even the guarantee of basic necessities for all. Many older people in the country live alone; a great many are dependent on friends or compassionate strangers with cars even to take them to the nearest physician; many are housebound.

There is, then, no question that what you have to give is needed. There is no dearth of things to do—full-time, part-time, occasionally, in a position of leadership, taking the initiative, or as a follower. The question is, What do you want to do, and how do you make your choices? Finally—and this is not unreasonable on your part to ask—what will be your compensations?

Rewards of Volunteering

Although the glorified rural paradise of our fathers is a thing of the past—if it ever existed—genuine neighborliness brings rewards in the country that are not possible in the detached, impersonal atmosphere of a city, even though simplicity and serenity may exist only on the surface of a rural community. The same passions and same dissensions can reign in small towns as in big ones, and it may not be possible to hide them so closely as in a metropolis. Yet there is an advantage in being close to problems and to those who have them; you view them differently. You can see their causes and results as you can never do without really great effort in a many-sided city. In short, you can be more important to your neighbors. There are also other compensations.

You will have a personal identification with the people you live among. They will respect your experience and your wisdom because they will probably know more about your background, even if they are not on close social terms with you, than your neighbors ever could in megalopolis. The area will be small enough, even if it is countywide, for you to investigate through established agencies, or even by yourself, what needs to be done. You can almost always choose your own kind and the extent of your participation without fear of so much competition that you will feel unnecessary. There is always work enough to go around, as well as a continuing need for leaders.

There is also tremendous satisfaction in knowing you can make your influence really felt. Newspapers and the other communications media—radio, television, magazines—are all more significant than in a city of many distractions. Both the letter columns, news space, and discussion time on the air will be more available to you for comments or suggestions than what you could secure in metropolitan dailies or on city radio and television stations.

You can contribute further by helping to keep governmental and elected officials on their toes, prodding them when they seem lethargic, reminding them of their obligations. Because the areas they cover permit you to stand out as an individual—which is possible only when the total population is small—you can have influence on committees, with county commissioners, with town councils when you learn enough to know their right from wrong. For instance, the dignified man with white hair who stopped one elected official to tell him that old man J. had been able to leave his isolated farmhouse for the first time in several years because a group from the neighborhood Center went after him and brought him to participate in an old-time quilting bee, had something more in mind. It was not lost on the person he was talking to that the meeting had had to be held in a drafty schoolhouse, and that the underlying purpose of the story was to get him to vote for funds to build or remodel a better meeting place. Thus, the biblical admonition of being mindful of your brother seems to have more chance of realization in rural areas than in large cities because your words and your acts carry more weight.

It is a common fallacy that in the "good old days" this need to take strong action was not necessary. The facts are that the good old days were not always so good. Moreover, there is everywhere a shamefaced readiness to face the fact now that rural pockets of dire poverty do exist and must be wiped out. If you are a newcomer, once you have settled down to rural life, find out what *you* can do. If you are a long-time resident, you may have to make a greater effort to be objective about conditions you may take for granted.

What You Can Do to Help

It is quite probable that you will find more outlets for what you know, and perhaps a much warmer welcome, than you ever would in a city of a million indifferent inhabitants. Toys need to be repaired for an orphanage, sewing has to be done for migrants or county infirmaries, nursing homes and homes for the aged—as in the city, good, bad, and in between—all need the warmth of personal visits and a person who cares.

Does the local Red Cross chapter need voluntary workers for its county fund-raising drive? Could your small town have a new library, or your church a new parish house, or the old people's home better furniture, or the Boy Scouts better equipment? If *you* could get more townspeople or farmers interested in such praiseworthy projects, there would never be a time when you felt the weight of years. Even if you became permanently housebound, or temporarily weather-bound, you still could find some charitable organization that would be glad for you to take on some jobs at home.

In a number of parts of the United States there are pilot or demonstration projects, some funded for a limited life by a foundation or a Federal grant, others set up in cooperation with private or state agencies on a semi-permanent or permanent basis. These projects are designed to help people in rural areas solve their own and other people's problems. If they do not exist where you are, try to find out what is happening elsewhere; it's not impossible that by acting as the catalyst you could bring them to your part of the country.

THE OREGON SELF-HELP PROGRAM

In Oregon the "comunity self-help program" is designed to make use of the capabilities of older residents for the purpose of revitalizing the lives of other people (and at the same time benefit themselves). There may be more—or fewer—possibilities where you live, but the list of potential services outlined in the application for a Federal grant is indicative of both the need and the various ways a person no longer young can still be a valuable asset.

In the Oregon request for the grant this statement was made (certainly applicable throughout the United States):

Communities need to utilize more effectively the older person as a resource in the community. Some of these persons would make ex-

97

cellent leaders of 4H and other youth groups, teachers for the very young homemakers, and "grandparents" for pre-school children.

Oregon has acted on that assumption. The project inaugurated by the Cooperative Extension Service of the U.S. Department of Agriculture, in cooperation with Oregon State University, envisages activities that could be carried out by older men and women for the benefit of every age group. This is a glimpse of some of them:

Youth in a 4-H club [previously organized by the Extension Service] might "adopt" an older person to visit and assist with small tasks such as running errands, mowing the lawn, etc. The older person in turn might teach club members some specific skill as woodworking or sewing. [Note this healthy tit for tat.]

A Neighborhood Youth Corps enrollee [one of the Office of Economic Opportunity projects] might receive the one-to-one support he needs to succeed on a job from a retired business man or woman. The older person might help locate the part-time job needed, and continue regular visits with both the youth and the employer to help the former develop acceptable work attitudes and to develop the employer's understanding of the youth's need for patient encouragement and recognition.

A disadvantaged family [located by an extension agent] might receive help and encouragement needed to relate to society from an elderly person adopted as a grandparent. Children in a fatherless home would particularly benefit from an adopted grandfather who might take them picnicking or fishing as well as share his masculine skills and values.

And so on.

That these ideas are considerably more than theory is illustrated by this concrete example.

Willamette City's two 4-H "Happy Stitchers Clubs" (one is all boys) was fortunate enough to have Mrs. Josie Holms as a leader. Retirement after twenty years as an elementary schoolteacher did not slow down Mrs. Holms's pace. As she says, she "got roped in young" as a 4-H forestry club leader. She admits to mixed feelings of sympathy and impatience for people who think they are "too busy" or "can't do this or that." "Anyone," says Mrs. Holms, "who enjoys youngsters can lead a 4-H Club successfully."

The key word, of course, is "enjoy." You may not enjoy working with boys and girls, but there are many other things to do, because, as one rural expert pointed out, "Whatever exists is apt to be diffuse, sporadic, and minimal, demonstrating the need for an organized, coordinated, whole-hearted effort by any individual who loves his fellow-man."

THE STATE OF WASHINGTON PLAN

The Council on Aging of Washington State cites an impressive list of eleven hundred older men and women, some of whom engage in more than one rural activity that adds to the happiness and well-being of other people. The gamut of what they do runs from membership in a telephone reassurance team, which keeps in contact with the isolated, to acting as leaders in county councils.

Here are just some of the ways older men and women in Washington (the state, not the capital) are demonstrating they can fill many types of posts. Any one of them offers a suggestion for adaptation to your own community, or may already exist. (The list is alphabetical, not in order of importance in the minds of either the givers or the recipients.)

Class instructors. This covers a wide variety of use of skills, from bowling, arts and crafts, and music, to conducting study groups for people of all ages.

Clerical work and bookkeeping. In Washington, as elsewhere, older men and women work in agencies that find them valuable adjuncts. They do addressing, filing, typing, and many other kinds of skilled and unskilled office work.

Entertaining. This is another flexible word. Individuals who play or sing may go by themselves or with a group to visit nursing homes, retirement homes, prisons, orphanages, hospitals. But there is also a nationally known orchestra, composed of retired professional musicians that performs in institutions as well as concert halls.

99

Friendly visiting. Calling on shut-ins in their homes or an institution is no different in the country areas than in a busy city. In Washington many do it under supervision of a local council on aging, a multiple-purpose senior center, the American Red Cross, or even a library.

General community service. This phrase covers such skills as knitting, sewing, woodworking, which county extension agents call on older men and women to offer. They also find use for them in safety and accident teaching programs, in home delivery of meals to the temporarily or permanently homebound, and as leaders of various types of recreation.

Host and hostess. An outgoing person finds gratification in a post in one or another type of senior citizen center, club, or lounge. Sometimes the host and hostess help serve food; occasionally it is prepared by them. More often they serve on the reception line, greeting newcomers, making old ones welcome, giving information about services in the community, or helping publicize events.

Repair work. This is badly needed work in many areas, particularly for those who live alone, are enfeebled, or isolated. Sometimes it means the difference between going into an institution and being helped to remain in one's own home. Many of Washington's volunteer handymen and carpenters make renovations or repairs in senior citizen centers or in offices of the council on aging.

Telephone service. This is something even the homebound or housebound can do. In Washington this reassurance service on a daily basis for the homebound is done under supervision of a center, a welfare agency, or a church, to avoid duplication.

Transportation. This is another elastic word. It may mean taking young people to visit elderly shut-ins to bring a breath of the juvenile world to them and to help bridge the generation gap; or it may involve walking or driving with older men and women, so they can make use of recreational facilities or go shopping; or it may mean an occasional trip to accompany them to the hospital or to a physician, or a regular arrangement so they can go to church or to club meetings.

Friendly Visiting

Because the problems that an aged couple or an isolated individual, feeble or ill, face in the country are much more acute than elsewhere, the role of "friendly visitor" is particularly important. Our country, heavily populated as it is, still has many people living in isolated areas in the mountains, or in regions where in many instances they are snowbound or swamp-bound for months.

A representative of the Farmers Union, which has interested itself in this acute problem, said during hearings of a Congressional Committee, "It is in rural areas where a special effort must be made to reach isolated individuals to do friendly visiting, personal telephoning, and provide social activities.

If person-to-person aid appeals to you, apply to the local nursing association, a social service agency, a recreation facility, the county welfare department, or county extension agent. You would be working under their trained supervision. This is one example: In the Rocky Mountains where there are nearly 10,000 mountain foot passes, much snow, and very low temperatures, older people can, and have, died alone. But that was before the Friendly Visitors and Transportation Service was started by the Northwest Colorado Visiting Nurse Association. Now visitors drawn from the general public make personal calls on all isolated older men and women at least once a week and keep in touch with them daily by telephone. When necessary, they are brought to the county seat for doctor's or hospital visits, to the bank or to transact some other business. One of the enthusiastic group of volunteers which makes this possible is a seventy-four-year-old retired miner; another is the ex–town marshal of a Colorado village (population 666).

Even where nature is not so rugged the occasional visit of someone interested can fill an important community need. To ascertain the facts the Farmers Union sponsored the pilot project CASA in Arkansas. (The initials stand for "Community Action for Senior Arkansans.") The project has attracted wide national and congressional attention because it highlights a situation only too prevalent in other parts of the country, plus the fact that it has demonstrated that capable older adults can help their less vigorous and more isolated peers.

In Arkansas men and women in the upper age brackets were sought out and hired (at minimum wages) to seek out aging people in out-of-the-way places and offer them practical help when needed.

The size of the problem (which exists in every state to a greater or less degree) is indicated by these figures: Several thousand older men and women were visited. Their age range was sixty-five to a hundred and four. The average age of these individuals was seventy-three, and their average income less than $950 yearly. The CASA visitors found that nearly 60 percent were in poor health, 36 percent lived in substandard housing, and many had not seen another human being in weeks, sometimes months.

If you want to know how the problem was met, or about other progressive attempts to conquer problems in rural areas, write the National Farmers Union. (One of its forward-looking projects is the "Green Thumbs" program, Federally financed, which is beautifying many barren areas.) Address

Executive Director,
Senior Member Council
National Farmers Union
1012 14th St., N.W.
Washington, D.C. 20005

The Holton Experiment

If you live in what you think is an agreeable small village not too far from city comforts, if you think your own age or lack of experience in community life prevent your participation in community affairs, take note of what happened in Holton, Kansas.

Holton has a population of about three thousand people, about one-fourth of whom are past their sixty-fifth birthday. You would probably consider it, as do its inhabitants, an average small town, U.S.A. What happened in Holton was the development of a research project whose objective was to find out not if older people *could* contribute something to the rural society in which they lived, but if they did, how it would affect their own morale and well-being.

The Holton project was a serious research effort, supported by the National Institute of Mental Health, and supervised by staff members assigned by the University of Kansas. Its chief purpose was to establish means of finding out whether a typical small town's older residents could be interested in a community project they themselves might initiate, and if so, what affect it would have on them, on the community, and on rural life in general.

The demonstration-project period was three years. Holton was chosen (after a careful survey of other places) because it was considered a representative Kansas rural community. It began with a survey, supervised by University of Kansas professional staff members, which uncovered not only a great array of diverse talents but the knowledge that the town's older inhabitants were making far too little use of them. Then action began—slowly at first.

In consultation with other civic organizations (and the town had a full share) the name "Neighbors United" was chosen by Holton's older citizens themselves. It was not just another "Golden Age Club." The town already had that. Neighbors United was organized as a voluntary older citizens' group, backed by leaders in the church and other community organizations. Its members were to decide on the forms of service that would be most useful in their rural county. When they did, they worked side by side with younger folk and with every type of civic organization. They took the lead in some tasks and became active members of teams in others. Everything was accomplished under the direction of the Executive Board of Neighbors United, whose members ranged in age from thirty to seventy-eight. During the three-year demonstration period much was undertaken that was technically (and sometimes, politically) difficult, but the jobs, once decided on, were carried through to completion. The results proved to the satisfaction of Holton's older population and the doubting Thomases in all groups, that it *is* possible for people of all ages to work well together and make genuinely valuable civic contributions that benefit not only the individuals who participate but the entire population. This is what they were able to do:

1. Their principal project was a community beautification program. It won not only statewide publicity but inspired local admiration and efforts. Older people took the lead and were the chief workers.

2. They established a Friendly Visitor service for the homebound, both young and old.

3. They made a countywide survey of urgent needs, and compiled lists of resources that existed to meet them.

103

4. They investigated the possibilities of a handyman service to reach the isolated, a counseling program, and a Head-Start program.

5. Finally Neighbors United assumed responsibility for initiating organization of a program to be funded by the Office of Economic Opportunity, designed to serve three neighboring counties.

Neighbors United was not just a slogan. Members worked actively with these organizations (and you will find them, or their equivalents, in any similar setting).

The American Legion
The Chamber of Commerce
The Golden Age Club
The Home Demonstration Unit
The Lions Club
The Ministerial Alliance
The Old Settlers' Association
The Pilot Club
The Parent-Teachers Association
The Rotary Club
The United Fund Campaign
The Veterans of Foreign Wars

If you wonder whether the supervision by professional social workers was the prop that sustained them during the three-year demonstration period and the reason for the success of Neighbors United, obviously it certainly was a great help. But pilot projects are designed to show what can and cannot be done. When the demonstration ended the Executive Board (remember it has both young and old among its deciding voices) voted unanimously that Neighbors United should become a permanent organization—on its own.

In the sedate language of one of the final official reports, "It appears that aging residents can actively and adequately fill a 'community participant' role."

Where to Offer Your Own Help

If you are an old-timer in the country you will know that frequently you will have to rely on informal resources or those less well organized than in a large city. They will not be so handily listed in a directory or in a community council office.

If you want to enlarge the scope of the contribution you may be making, or if you are a newcomer eager to become a real part of the community in which you expect to spend your later years, you will need to know your county, what it has and what it does not have to meet the needs of the population. If you let it be known you have interest to give and time to spare, do not let either be gobbled up until you have consulted the chief avenues of information, the sources through which you can find out, reliably, what is being carried on and what is projected for the future.

THE ROLE OF THE EXTENSION SERVICE

Whether you want to stay in the background or take a leadership role, the one agency you should not fail to consult is the Cooperative Extension Service, the educational branch of the U.S. Department of Agriculture. It is represented by county agricultural agents and/or home economists in every rural county of our nation. There are some three thousand offices in the United States, and you will find the nearest one at your own county seat. It will be listed in the telephone book under some such title as "Extension Service," "U.S. Cooperative Extension Service," or "——— County Extension Service."

Part of the function of Extension workers is to further community relationships and community development. Therefore, if you want to find out anything that concerns the program of another agency, it is highly likely that one of the county agents can give you an honest appraisal of what it has done and what it is capable of doing, and concretely, whether there is a good place in its work for you.

It is the county extension agent who goes into the shanty-towns, the hollows, and the most isolated swampy areas to reach young and old. "Professors in the field," someone has called these professional men and women who live among the people they work with. They include specialists in agriculture, home economics, financial management, youth work, and many other fields. In addition, they are skilled planners who work with local citizens of every age to set up projects to meet recognized needs.

Do not hesitate to talk freely to the one you meet. From its earliest beginnings the U.S. Cooperative Extension Service has had a basic philosophy that governs its work with the older generation. Its agents consider older men and women simply a specific segment of the total population, and aging a normal part of existence. It is taken for granted that all life's experiences are a preparation for growing old, and that if you have had the good luck to arrive at the stage when you have acquired wisdom, you ought to be willing to pass it along.

The Cooperative Extension Service in every state is connected with land-grant colleges or universities. (See Appendix.) Sometimes there is more than one in a state. Many have begun to work with state commissions or councils on aging. Because of the growing numbers of people over sixty-five, constantly augmented, some already have specialists in this field on their staff and are sponsoring demonstration programs to enable people with more leisure than they had in their on-the-job years to take an active part in community affairs. Their offices are sometimes housed with the Extension Services, but if not, the agent you talk to will know if such a project is under way in your area.

You may find your most rewarding involvement, however, may be in working with the Extension Service itself. As an integral part of the U.S. Department of Agriculture, its objective is to help anybody to obtain any assistance he needs. In addition, it works with rural areas' development committees composed of local groups to organize programs. This covers everything from hot meals for the needy bedbound, to housing loans for the more fortunate. In spite of the thousands of staff members through the nation, there are never enough. So the Cooperative Extension Service not only needs but gives a hearty welcome to volunteers. There are vacancies on committees for good people, and among its numerous educational programs, one is in leadership training. But whether you decide you prefer to work in its nutrition program, or with a 4-H club of youngsters, or help in the vital role of aiding elderly people living on limited incomes in out-of-the-way spots, there will be a place for you. By volunteering you will help the relatively limited professional staff reach more people; by cooperating with these useful public servants you will not only benefit others but will be making a greater use of your own potential.

Information regarding county or statewide programs, local resources, and a publications list can be obtained at the county seat, or from the nearest land-grant college or university. Or for a view of the national program and how it affects your area write directly to

Human Development and Human Relations Department
Cooperative Extension Service
U.S. Department of Agriculture
Washington, D.C. 20250

THE CURRENT ROLE OF CHURCHES

If you prefer to use the more traditional forms of service organizations of your own youthful recollection, you could not do better than to get in touch with any pastor or priest in the county. For churches still play relatively a much more prominent role in villages than in metropolitan areas, and on the whole, probably reach a higher percentage of the population. Any minister of any faith is a good person to consult. You need not be a member of his congregation, and it is not likely any pressure will be put on you to join it when you make your queries. But he will know his community, usually in depth, and will be able to refer you to the leaders in a particular organization that may be functioning well, or that needs aid to do so. If you do not know what you would like to do, he can help you to the extent of telling you what is lacking or which group is handicapped by not having enough interested people, and perhaps even assist you to make a choice.

SEE THE COUNTY WELFARE DEPARTMENT

If you have already made up your mind that you want to do your share in the national struggle to wipe out poverty pockets, or if you would just like a thumbnail picture of what is being done to combat them, go to the county seat and see the county welfare director. He will not only know the names and the personalities of community leaders, but he will be familiar with organizations of every kind—

107

economic, educational, political, among others—as well as individuals working in the field of private and public social welfare. You will find that there is no one pattern of county welfare offices. Your own county welfare director may combine in his person the role of administrator, caseworker, and community planner; or he may have the administrative and coordinating role in a department that provides a wide variety of services.

STATE OR COUNTY COUNCILS OR COMMISSIONS

If you are edging into the sixties or are already there, write or call your state commission on aging. (See Appendix for exact name and address.) Ask specifically what is being done *for* and *by* people in your age bracket and request a local referral source. Many states have county commissions on aging; several others have developed arrangements with the U.S. Department of Agriculture's state extension services. In those cases leadership in county organization and education may be helped through employment of a specialist on aging; frequently this person's headquarters (as in Louisiana, North Carolina, and Texas) will be in the offices of the extension service.

Do not make the mistake of thinking the county or state council or commission on aging is interested only in the needy or the forlorn. One of the by-products of working with either is the possibility of meeting and getting to know interesting, worthwhile people. It is quite possible that joining with them will make your retirement take on overtones that may enrich your life beyond initial expectations.

MULTIPURPOSE CENTERS

Although you may never before have thought of entering one of the many varieties of so-called senior citizen centers, belonging to one that is truly a multipurpose center in a rural area has advantages. For one thing it is likely to be a place in which you will meet your contemporaries, no matter what their financial rating is. For another, however small, it is likely to have a card file that indexes the talents, skills, and interests of its members. In addition to social activities— they usually cover a wide range—it is therefore equipped to answer requests from all kinds of rural agencies for help, such as the American National Red Cross, the tuberculosis association, the cancer fund drive.

Multipurpose centers in the country are not as outwardly imposing and not as professionally staffed as they are in a city. But this is sometimes one of their assets. A rural county may be able to have only one center, opening its doors one or two days a week, or even for just a weekly four or five hour period. But because its work depends largely on the aid of volunteers with talent, warm hearts, and ingenuity, it is usually a lively, interesting place. It may be housed in an old opera house (the first home of the center in Yellow Springs, Ohio), or may be established in an abandoned freight office (as was done in St. Johns, Michigan).

But how they came about is more important than their physical set-up. Most have grown out of the determination of men and women bent on disproving the fallacious notion that because they have achieved a certain chronological age they should sit back and let others work for them and the place they call home.

If you have any doubt that the nearest multipurpose center in your own vicinity is worth investigating, consider what happened in St. Johns, Michigan (population 5,636). When an old freight office was renovated and felicitously renamed the "Drop-in Center," this was the comment in the *Farm Journal* in December, 1967: "It's a product of the youthful zest of the county's old folks who decided to put their own resources to work solving some of their income, health, and recreation problems."

But the Drop-In Center does considerably more than that, because all of Clinton County benefits by its programs. Its visiting service provides companionship for patients in the county infirmary and for individuals who are homebound. Its volunteers staff a referral and employmet service. Others plan social events, maintain a band, and keep a bowling league in operation. Because pressure was exerted by its civic-minded members, local zoning laws and building codes have been modified for the better. Furthermore, when they are not using it, the Drop-In Center is rented to the town recreation department for youth and community activities.

If there is no such center where you live there are a great many community organizations that will help you organize one. They already know that these senior citizen centers, or clubs, have one thing in common everywhere. They enhance self-esteem, overcome loneliness, and broaden social and civic horizons. If you do not need this bolster, perhaps your neighbors do. Nor need you be wealthy yourself or stand back because such a center has no prospective building of its own. A random survey of where they are found in rural areas in just one state includes (a) a private home, (b) headquarters of a lodge, (c) a hall rented out by a veterans organization, (d) a church, (e) a school house, (f) the city hall.

The county commission on aging or its state office, the county welfare department, and the county Extension Service will all be interested in helping to launch any venture like this which will encourage people (regardless of social and economic background) to remain active in the community.

Working for the Disabled

There is a special section of the rural population which has suffered hardship because there are comparatively few of the usual facilities found in cities to aid them. These are the thousands of men, women, and children crippled by disabling diseases. The problem is particularly acute in finding employment for those who can and want to work, or to train them in jobs they can perform for pay. The type of workshops and office and factory training possibilities possible in large cities are practically nonexistent.

To remedy this situation the President's Committee on Employment of the Handicapped determined in 1968 that henceforth the rural disabled should be included in its sphere of action. Its state commissions and committees and its municipal ones all call on volunteers to help further its work to make the handicapped independent through rehabilitation. Its present Rural Areas Committee, with headquarters in the national office in Washington, D.C., was organized to form state, county, and local committees in small towns and villages. Their purpose will be to find ways of rehabilitating men and women who want to lead independent lives, if possible, free from charity.

Whatever your own experience has been, if you have a compassion-

110

ate heart, you can be used in this program, and perhaps even be able to shape it. Success locally and nationally will be measured by the interest and devotion of those willing to work in this almost neglected field. Training disabled adults so they can hold jobs, and then finding the job that matches the capacity, is not easy in any area and is especially difficult in the country. For that reason the work will be challenging.

The Governor's Committee on Employment of the Handicapped is usually located in the capital city. You can write to ask what you can do to help. Or address your query directly to

Chairman, Rural Areas Committee
President's Committee on Employment of the Handicapped
Washington, D.C. 20210

As the Secretary of the Rural Areas Committee points out, "This is a program designed to bring a little more happiness and hope into the lives of the handicapped."

THE MINNESOTA STORY

Anyone who really wants to know how conditions can be bettered in rural areas, and what he himself can actually accomplish, should read, from cover to cover, this booklet:

A Rural County Cares for Its Aging
Case Study #17
U.S. Department of Health, Education, and Welfare, Administration on Aging (revised 1967)
Superintendent of Documents
U.S. Printing Office, Washington, D.C.
20402. $.15

This is the story of what happened in Aitkin County, Minnesota. It can happen anywhere if there are enough dedicated people willing to exert themselves to arouse community spirit. The requisite spark can be supplied by anyone at any age.

Like many other areas, Aitkin County in mid-central Minnesota (a state largely rural) has a population of older people out of propor-

111

tion to the sum total of its inhabitants. Most of them have low incomes, and many lives in isolation. Younger, spryer people have often moved away.

What to do to make life less desolate for the elderly in this unfertile area, which covers almost two thousand square miles dotted with lakes and bogs, had long been a challenge to the state. Previous attempts to alleviate the lot of the almost two thousand men and women over sixty-five there had not been successful.

It was not until 1959 that the Minnesota Governor's Citizens Council on Aging resolved to use part of a Federal grant to see what could be accomplished with the aid of local citizens. But when the Council's consultant went into the town of Aitkin (the county seat) he found its people, he said, "generally depressed, overwhelmed with problems, and cynical about plans for the elderly."

Neither he nor the few people he found to help him were willing to take this attitude as the final answer. They talked and they argued, and they refused to be discouraged. Above all, they *worked*. This is what was happening just four years later.

A Senior Center had been organized. It was located in the renovated basement of a church whose superstructure had been destroyed by fire. Its Saturday night dances were drawing people like Mr. W., aged ninety-two, though he lived twelve miles away. Aitkin is a tiny town (then its population was only 2,000), yet some of the eighty men and women who were coming regularly to enjoy the weekly gaiety at the Center lived thirty to forty miles from this small county seat.

But that was only a beginning. By 1967 the dances were taking place twice a month and had had to be moved to a larger building to accommodate the crowds. In addition there was a daily program under the leadership of volunteers. The one-day-a-week arts and crafts classes and hobby sales were flourishing; the Over-60 Choir sang weekly at two nursing homes in the county. In addition the Senior Center had become the focus of other community activity. The association for retarded children used it mornings for classes; the Girl Scouts, the hospital auxiliary, and the mental health association held their meetings in it. In addition, four Golden Age Clubs had been organized in remote areas, and meetings were held once a month. For those who drove, or were driven to them from a distance of fifteen to twenty miles, they represented practically the only time it was possible to visit with friends and engage in programs that promote fellowship.

It may be that you live where such acute problems do not need to be faced. But it is worthwhile remembering that Aitkin's success was made possible only by the vision, persistence, and determination of a few older men and women. They were backed, to be sure, by an understanding state organization on aging and had the advantage of the tireless enthusiasm of the local director of the welfare department. But there was no power, no money, and no big names to win a following. And the organization that named itself the Aitkin County Citizens Committee on Aging for a long time faced apathy or actual hostility on the part of the younger set.

No one would deny that a good part of the success was due to the resolution and the untiring work of two people. If you ever feel discouraged when you try to make your own voice felt in some cause dear to you, take heart from what they did.

Mrs. Malvick was already in her seventies when she began her vigorous campaign on behalf of her neighbors. She was the wife of a semi-retired building construction man, and their home was on a lake several miles from the county seat.

Mr. Arens, then in his sixties, was the Aitkin postmaster. Long before anybody else had thought it possible, Mr. Arens felt there should be easily accessible places for older people where they could follow mutual interests and enjoy companionship. He was haunted by the memory of his aged parents, living alone in their farmhouse with no callers and no outside interests. When he first began to talk about his idea most people thought he was an impractical idealist. But when the county committee was finally organized, Mr. Arens became its first chairman. His dream had become a solid reality.

Mrs. Malvick, too, was determined that older people should have the opportunity to live lives of dignity and purpose. She worked long days and nights trying to overcome indifference on the part of both old and young, raising funds, sometimes almost dollar by dollar, finding volunteer leaders, supervising activities, and making plans for the future (which included eventually a hotly fought battle to bring low-income public housing to Aitkin, which many of the townspeople did not feel was needed and did not want.)

Mrs. Malvick literally has driven her car thousands of miles over rough back country roads, visiting potential leaders, or just making her rounds of calls on lonely old people. Also, she has twice served as chairman of the Aitkin County Citizens Committee on Aging.

The final lesson of the Aitkin County story is that people can become aroused about any good cause at any age. And if they are determined enough they can enlist others' support and achieve a goal if it is worthwhile in spite of negativism and discouragement. Naturally one has to have a capacity for warmth and empathy to deal with varying individuals, whether they are recalcitrant officials or lackadaisical citizens. In rural neighborhoods reliability is just as much respected and perhaps appreciated more than in the impersonal atmosphere of a big city.

It is not necessary to rely on paid or elected officials or highly trained professional people to get all this world's work done. We tend increasingly to rely so much on the professional community that we are in danger of losing the unique American tradition of volunteer help, which was one of the notable features of the rural communities of our fathers. Dr. Saul Silverman said it in these striking words when he addressed Home Economists of the U.S. Department of Agriculture's Extension Service: "In the end, the helping relationship does not belong to the professionals; it does not belong to the psychiatrists; it belongs to caring people."

Chapter VI

What National Organizations Have to Offer

Possibly you are among the many who believe that charity begins at home. There is nothing wrong in that point of view. However, you can find additional satisfaction in participating in your community's affairs if at the same time you play a role in accomplishing some national, or even international, goal.

This dual aim is neither incompatible nor impossible. It is a fallacy to believe that policies of national or international organizations emanate from a faraway base and therefore nobody in the hinterland can influence them. The basic purposes of any organization have to be carried out, of course, and you do not become a member of a local unit of one if you do not believe in furthering them. Nevertheless, programs in specific localities, as well as the financial campaigns that support them, are frequently based on decisions made by local citizenry and carried out according to their wishes. In addition a community may be chosen, or is self-chosen, to be the "guinea pig" for a pilot or experimental program that on completion may bring a whole chain of national reactions in its wake.

Furthermore, you can become interested in something even of worldwide importance because prominent agencies of every kind have regional or branch offices throughout the country, sometimes in every state, often in major urban centers, and even at the county seat in rural areas.

The influence that a local demonstration project can exert is well illustrated by "Helpmate," launched by a branch (called a Section) of the National Council of Jewish Women in Philadelphia in the early 1960's. Its purpose was to find out whether older men and women wanted to be and could be active in some kind of community service. Headquarters was one modest room. Hundreds of retired men and women of all creeds and races flocked to register in what was actually a volunteer service bureau organized for people over sixty. The average age of the enrolees was seventy, and their occupations varied from ex-scrubwoman to ex-admiral.

The success of Helpmate spurred other local Sections of the National Council of Jewish Women to attempt the same idea. Very soon people like the retired architect in Essex County, New Jersey, were using their talents for a good cause. (He advised an interracial group in the building of a new church.) In Stamford, Connecticut, through the Council's "RSVP" (Retired Stamford Volunteer Personnel) an agile older woman was recruited to give dance lessons to retarded teen-agers—and so it went.

Though the pilot projects ended their demonstration period in 1966, many Sections continue to carry theirs on. But the greatest importance of the all-out three-year demonstrations was that they secured vast publicity locally and sometimes nationally which reinforced the very sound idea that people in the upper-age brackets are, by and large, able to contribute and want to contribute effectively wherever they live. The result of just that one period of experimentation is bound to be felt in the national ripples it aroused, reinforcing the idea of a "National Community Service Corps," which would enroll older men and women throughout the United States. As Mrs. Fred Weiser, herself a volunteer, and Assistant Treasurer of the

National Council of Jewish Women at the time, pointed out at a Congressional hearing,

> The initial findings of our pilot projects are only a first step. This is one of the special functions that a voluntary organization is best able to perform—it can take the pioneering steps, make the first mistakes; and find out what to do and what not to do.

You need not wait, either, for a program that commits our country to a concept of community service. If you are still uncommitted, become aware of some of the advantages of enrolling under the banner of a national or international organization.

Advantages of National Affiliation

There are distinct benefits in becoming part of an organization that has already won renown for "good works," whether they be in health, welfare, education, politics, or any other field.

First of all, you have the assurance that you are not joining a fly-by-night organization. Too many people, eager just "to be doing something useful," are ignorant (or indifferent) when it comes to the cause they join, provided they know, sometimes too vaguely, that it is reputed to be a good one. If you are inclined to be more discriminating, it will be worth the time you give to it to investigate some national organization's local branch and find out how closely it is carrying out its national purpose, and how much it reflects your own views.

There is also a deep gratification in realizing that even if you never leave your home base, you can still be part of agencies with international affiliations which link their local branches to the common concerns of individuals in other nations. To be part of such an organization means that one has the opportunity to see beyond the boundaries of his own community and have a chance to realize— and to work for—that concept that the world is one.

There is another advantage, even closer home. If you affiliate with an organization that has long-established programs, it is at least a quasi guarantee that what you do locally to further them will be in the common good. This does not mean you cannot continue to be loyal to a struggling local endeavor, but it does mean that a local branch of a well-established national or international agency, with years of experience behind it, will function with something more than good intentions. Often, by joining one with a social action program of national significance, you can help exert influence, both overt and covert, which has a chance of resulting in Federal or state advances in legislation.

The range and scope before you is as wide as any interest you may have. If you are interested in working with young people, or with those in your own age group; if you would like to further the idea of universal peace or brotherhood; or if you prefer to join the crusade for better housing, better interracial relations, or in conquering some other urban or rural blight; or even if you simply want to add a bit to the world's knowledge of its geography or its unknown outer or inner space, you may be sure that many others in the United States feel as you do. Some of them, somewhere, will have surely banded together to promote their aims. (If you do know one that has no local membership group with which you can affiliate, get in touch with its national headquarters and find out what needs to be done to get like-minded people to join you. You will be given ample help to get started.)

At a time of life when you may prefer to curtail your activities or channel them in one or a few directions, look for the organization that represents your chief interests. You will be more successful if you understand the way national organizations function. Roughly, they fall into these classes:

1. Few provide help to individuals locally except through a member group affiliated with the national one.

Example. The Child Study Association of America renders direct service only in the New York metropolitan area where its headquarters are located. Its training programs for professionals are developed and carried out, however, with national and local agencies in all parts of the country. It also provides consultative service to community groups on a wide basis.

118

2. Another category of national organization has local membership groups to organize public opinion.

Example: The United Nations Association of the U.S.A. functions through three hundred chapters.

3. The third category is the most common, an association that acts as the national service body for local groups.

Example. This includes such widespread organizations as the YMCA's and YWCA's, or the various medical and health organizations that have local affiliates.

The variations on these themes are diverse, but in every case the organization will depend heavily on the interest and enthusiasm of volunteers, however widely scattered. For instance, the American Friends Service Committee and the National Association for Mental Health refer to themselves as "volunteer-centered" rather than "staff-centered." Hadassah, the women's branch of the Zionist organization, which supports various medical services in Israel, is even more specific. It officially states that volunteers operate its organization and that staff members, here and abroad, are hired to help them carry out its purposes.

Organization Off the Beaten Path

A common mistake the uninitiated make is to assume that all organizations with a national or international scope concern themselves with philanthropic, religious, health, or medical matters, or fall into the widely assorted group that promotes various types of education. These do command much attention and loom high in the scale of importance to all of us. Nevertheless, if something less usual appeals to you, there are new paths you can explore, equally respectable and worthwhile, and you can find them even if you live in a village.

For instance, you can be part of the international scene wherever you live. There are organizations that promote letter-writing to strangers overseas to foster brotherhood. Your vis-à-vis will be matched to you, if not in sex or age, in like interests. Or, more per-

119

sonally, if you have the time and opportunity to provide overnight or weekend hospitality or even a meal occasionally, or just want to show the town sights to someone from far away, you can widen your own horizon at the same time if you get in touch with the adviser to foreign students on the nearest college campus. Or your own chamber of commerce would be glad to know you are willing to be a host for a brief period to enable a foreign visitor to obtain real insight into how our democracy functions.

There are also international associations with local chapters which have programs of interest, and others with far-reaching plans to draw more Americans into their work. Representative ones include the following:

Institute of International Education
809 United Nations Plaza
New York, N.Y. 10017

United Nations Association of the U.S.A. Inc.
345 East 46th St., New York, N.Y. 10017

In addition, your local pastor or priest will know of his denomination's ventures in the foreign field and its links in your own community, for study or for support.

If you are interested in the world of science, you have the assurance that organizations of every kind carry on their work with casual acceptance of the fact that chronological aging, like other phenomena in nature, is a matter of individual differences. (Perhaps this is why professional scientists infrequently retire in the literal sense of that word; nor do they just fade away. The American Chemical Society, for instance, maintains a list of retired engineers and chemists who continue to be available for part-time or occasional work. The American Institute of Biological Sciences conducts an Emeritus Biologist program, and the American Psychological Association, among others, has a list of active older people who have no intention and no desire of becoming has-beens.) Such a climate of acceptance insures your welcome, even if you can do no more than help out in the office of a local nature museum (likely to be as undermanned as any other nonprofit agency).

Whether or not you have a background in some scientific field, or merely a laymen's hobby interest, the simplest way to discover what you can do is to write directly to the headquarters of the organization; you can find out whether it has a local affiliate, or if it has none, and what you can do, anyway. For instance, it does not require more than good eyes and a love of winged creatures to be a bird-watcher or a census-counter of the bird population in your area for the National Audubon Society. If conservation of this nation's resources is a consuming passion, the U.S. Fish and Wildlife Service can tell you what is and is not being done in your region, and what you can do to help a professional staff.

Any sizable public library will have this valuable directory:

Scientific and Technical Societies of the United States
Published by the National Academy of Sciences
2101 Constitution Ave, Washington, D.C. 20418
1968 edition, $12.50

To cite only one instance of how matter-of-factly you will be accepted for what you can do and know (not because you are classified in one or another age category), the American Association of Variable Star Observers is always looking for new people to aid in its work. This is a worldwide organization that carries on its important investigations chiefly with the aid of volunteers. Their main activity is to observe stars, estimate the changing brightness of certain of them, and then send their observations to Association headquarters. There their own and other findings are correlated, printed, and distributed to professional astronomers throughout the world.

All that is needed is good eyesight and some kind of instrument, which can be anything from binoculars to a telescope of any size. *Note:* Some people have continued this fascinating work up until their nineties, and others have just started when they entered their sixties.

The Director, a well-known astronomer, says practically, "The retired person has a great advantage over the working one in that he can stay up as late at night as he wishes; before dawn observations are of great value in extending the observing season by catching the variables as they are rising in the morning."

Watching the stars at any hour develops a sense of proportion about life's little annoyances. If you are interested, write to

American Association of Variable Star Observers
187 Concord Avenue, Cambridge, Massachusetts 02138

The Climate of Acceptance

What kind of reception will you receive? Are all national organizations aware of the potentialities of an older volunteer, or do attitudes differ from one agency to another?

In 1961 the call to action for the White House Conference on Aging contained this statement: "National voluntary organizations can make a unique contribution by providing older citizens with opportunities to remain active contributors to the national welfare."

It would be pleasant to record that after this Conference, which in many ways was a landmark in initiating action in the U.S.A., the eager older seeker after a useful role could find an open door. The truth is a little less glowing. Several years after the Conference of 1961 a meeting held in the headquarters of the National Council on Aging explored the experiences various nonprofit agencies had had in using older people as volunteers. This was the consensus reached by representatives of public and privately supported organizations:

National organizations are just beginning to move. . . . The most imaginative programming is being done on the local level. . . . Emphasis in current national programming is on recognition of the necessity for providing volunteer opportunities as an integral part of overall services, involvement of older adults in planning and administering the program and selective placement to ensure that the volunteer job yields the greatest enthusiasm.

When you put this in plain, unvarnished terms, it means that national organizations, like local ones, differ in their practices and in their attitudes. Your most specific information about any organization and your clue to its standing in your community comes from people already part of its volunteer corps in your own community. The names of local leaders will appear on letterheads or in its publicity.

If you prefer to do your own research, consult a volunteer service bureau if the opportunity arises, just as you would if you wanted any other community post. If you want to know about any national organization, you can always write for information. Their publicity departments prepare a wealth of material, free for the asking. An obliging librarian in your hometown may also have the time to route you to magazine articles through which major national and international organizations spread news of certain phases of their work.

In short, the difficulty is not in finding out about organizations; it is in making your choice, because without you and your peers most of them could not function at all. There are certain additional opportunities open to you, if you are willing and able, which go beyond the usual forms of community service. The following are representative:

1. National organizations sometimes carry on research on a limited local basis. If you have the background, you may be asked to help conduct local studies, do research, or formulate findings of a survey.

2. If you serve on a committee or board, one of your values to the national organization will be your ability to reflect local or regional points of view.

3. If you have writing or editorial ability, there is frequently an opportunity to express views in the organizational magazine, or write articles for general circulation in magazines or other communications media, no matter where you live.

4. You may lead voices in assent or dissent before legislatures or before Congressional hearings. *Examples:* Volunteers from the League of Women Voters are heard with respect by legislators everywhere; senatorial hearings concerned with matters such as the projected National Senior Citizens Service Corps have reflected views of older people in many organizations.

Your primary usefulness, of course, will be as an active member of a local group attempting to vitalize the mandates of the national organization. Here, as everywhere, the usual three R's are indispensable—regularity, reliability, and resourcefulness—plus the ability to accept suggestions from a professional staff, even when they lack your years or your experience.

Where to Look for Acceptance

To make things easier for yourself, take a look at a number of organizations that for years past have recognized that age in itself can be an asset.

For long before stress was laid on making use of the power latent in a mounting older population, certain national organizations, among them those engaged in molding the lives of our youth so they can meet adults responsibilities, had recognized the values older people can bring to problems in an unsettled world.

So a good place to begin your queries is among youth organizations. Most of the important ones are represented in the chief centers of population, and a great many in small centers. The following list, not all-inclusive, is suggestive of the wealth of opportunity in this area for an older generation.

THE BOY SCOUTS OF AMERICA

No Johnny-come-latelies in making use of the values of an older man, the Boy Scouts of America has already given its Fifty-year Veterans' Award to over six hundred who have served it well. Seventy-eight others have been similarly honored for fifty-five years of service. Considering that the Boy Scouts of America was founded in 1910, that means that as early as the second decade of this century the organization was acting on the assumption—before solemn studies had confirmed the fact elsewhere—that older people can exert a good influence on the young.

There is no age limit for any position held by a volunteer in the Boy Scouts. If hiking and camping as a Cubmaster or Scoutmaster become too strenuous, there are always other services needed which are just as meaningful. In Honolulu, for instance, Charles Lee, retired, has been active in scouting for many years. Now he renders equally valuable aid by maintaining all the records of training courses participated in by other, younger volunteers. Similarly, in

South Bend, Indiana, the former treasurer of a leading automobile factory gives part of his time in the office of the Boy Scout Council, supervising financial record-keeping.

Most older people, however, like most young ones, like to work directly with the boys. There are more than five hundred local Boy Scout Councils, and there are opportunities in them to work with one of three age groups, ranging from eight years to eighteen or so. You will not be in the minority if you decide to help any one of them; there are already more than one and a half million adult volunteers assisting nearly five thousand full-time professional leaders watch over six million of America's youngsters.

Regardless of age, the essential qualification is the ability to win the respect and confidence of the boys you will be associated with either as Cubmaster, Scoutmaster, or an Explorer Advisor. (This last category means working with young fellows of high school age.)

The post of merit badge counselor has special appeal to retired men who are experts in their own fields and can stimulate young people to follow their bent for either a stimulating hobby or a career. The range in this elective program, which comprises over a hundred and ten subjects, is from astronomy to zoology.

There are also leadership roles that call on the experience of older men in a variety of challenging ways.

Thousands of boys who might have had to do without the benefits of scouting have been able to enjoy it because Glenn Young was interested in them and the hundred or more adult leaders he has helped to recruit and train after he retired and moved to Tampa, Florida. He wasted no time trying to follow in Ponce de Leon's footsteps; he found his own fountain of youth in continuing the work he had begun in Minnesota in 1929. He did it so well in Duluth he was presented with the Silver Beaver Award for distinguished services to boyhood. When he retired to Florida he became a full-time worker, organizing boy scout units wherever he saw a need, reorganizing old ones when the original interest had waned. He is a volunteer who has followed that same pattern forty-four times and seems likely to go on doing it.

Similarly, in Parksburg, West Virginia, the spirit of '76 is not a historical reference but refers to Scoutmaster Don B. Lowe. Now a retired bank executive, he has led the First United Presbyterian Church's Troop 3 since it started more than a half-century ago. When his golden anniversary as a Scoutmaster was celebrated ex-scouts came from nineteen states to honor him. At his anniversary dinner he outlined plans for the scouting year ahead, the most ambitious being the rebuilding of a seawall and a boat dock; he is not interested in his past exploits.

To find out what is happening in your own community, call Boy Scout headquarters wherever you are, or write for information to national headquarters:

Boy Scouts of America
New Brunswick, New Jersey 08903

GIRL SCOUTS OF THE U.S.A.

The Girl Scouts of the United States of America has had a long and honorable history. It was founded in 1912 and chartered by Congress in 1950. But it was not until 1967 that it launched its own "older Americans" program in a joint venture with the U.S. Administration on Aging. The project was conceived as a partnership that would benefit both old and young. It envisioned a wide variety of useful services to the old by Girl Scouts, comprising three and a half million members in the age range from seven to seventeen years old. Girls who make regular visitors to the homebound, to nursing homes, and homes for the aged are part of the project, "Operation Granddaughter."

The reverse of the picture—"Adopted Grandmother"—is outlined in a leaflet produced for the Girl Scouts by the Administration on Aging. Its caption reads, "We need you to teach us what you have learned." Everywhere, it points out, there is an opportunity to assist Girl Scout troops become more informed, more mature, and more knowledgeable in such areas as home economics, consumer education, arts, crafts, community affairs, and general personality development. Older people (sometimes of both sexes) work with girls in one or more of the four age level groups, or with their young adult leaders.

If you think you would like to work with young people of different

126

races, creeds, nationalities, economic and geographical and social backgrounds; or if you have skills you can impart to them or to their leaders, the Girl Scout Councils in your community can use you. Here are some of the things you can do:

1. You can help with hobby shows, exhibits, home-making, share your travel experiences or other interests, or do career counseling.

2. You can be a teacher or a library aid, or help a Girl Scout troop find its own meaningful community project.

3. You can be the expert who helps Junior Girl Scouts in such avocations as needlecraft, raising pets, health and safety programs.

4. You can aid Cadette Girl Scouts in planning inter-troop or inter-council art festivals or a dramatic workshop.

5. If you have a background in any science you can help a leader of a Brownie troop nurture small girls' curiosity, or help Senior Girl Scouts plan a science fair.

6. If you know a foreign language you may be able to contribute to the preparation of girls and adults selected for international study or international exchanges.

7. You can give advice to girls on careers and colleges

If you prefer to work directly on behind-the-scenes organization you can join thousands of retired people who serve on Girl Scout council-wide committees involved in program planning, training, finances, and public relations. The end of all this is to develop character traits that will build leadership for our country and a sense of responsibility in young people. If you want to share what you know with the girls themselves, or help the staff in personnel, program services, training, publicity, or finances, apply to the Girl Scout Council in your own community. To find out more about policies, programs, and service opportunities, write

Girl Scouts of the U.S.A.
830 Third Ave., New York, N.Y. 10022

WORKING WITH TROUBLED YOUNGSTERS

If you have been disturbed by antisocial action carried on by restless young people, if you have tolerance of their follies and understanding of what provokes them, there are a number of organizations you can join which operate on a national basis. Most of them are eager to use the wisdom born out of experience with crises in your own youthful life.

It has been found that authority one step removed from legal discipline, shown by someone with no blood ties to the young troubled person, is often effective. It is also frequently true that when that person is a generation removed from parents or legal guardians he or she finds it easier to reach troublemakers or potential delinquents.

There is more than one organization attempting to cope with the unrest of adolescents today. Big Brothers, Inc. is one that is widely respected. It tries to guide boys away from antisocial behavior, and its network is nationwide. National headquarters sets no age limit for those who can fill the role of an adequate male figure in the life of a boy who lacks one. But be sure you know exactly what that means before you apply locally.

"Little Brothers" are neither potential criminals nor necessarily known to any juvenile court. They are boys between the ages of eight and seventeen who have shown symptoms sufficiently disturbing to come to the attention of some teacher or a social worker or a pastor. Behavior problems may show themselves in school failures, family conflict, gang activity or self-destructive tendencies; any one of these can lead to serious delinquency if unchecked. But if a boy can be reached early enough, he can usually be redirected into wholesome behavior patterns.

If you are a person with a stable personality, willing to take a few hours regularly each week to help youngsters, you will not have to assume any legal or financial responsibilities for them. Nor will you be left without guidance. Assignments are made by professional workers who select and match boys and men and who subsequently supervise their relationships. The matching is done on the basis of compatibility, and weight is always given to cultural, racial, religious, and social factors.

If you are drawn to this kind of role, remember that you are *not* expected to play the role either of a substitute probation officer, pastor, physician, psychiatrist, or social worker. You are not expected —or permitted—to come into a boy's life to moralize or lecture him. You will be there to fill a void, an emotional vacuum, which needs filling with affection, sympathy, understanding, and the guidance that is important to any youngster anywhere. Although it is fun to attend sporting events with an eager young companion, share his interests in hobbies or amusements, go to the circus, the theater, or to church with him, your chief reward will be an intangible one. Your work will be done when you have guided him sufficiently far along the road to know he is not going to need you any longer to keep out of trouble, though you may (and this does happen) remain in contact with him over the years.

Each case is different, but this one will suffice to tell you that an "adopted grandfather" can sometimes do what a younger person cannot.

In the files of the Big Brothers in a Western city there is the story of one ten-year-old. Because of bitter memories, he failed to respond in the way it was hoped he would to the young man assigned as his Big Brother. But Billy's attitude changed remarkably when an elderly man took over the task of giving him the affection and companionship he so sorely needed. Mr. X. became the substitute grandfather the child had never known instead of the substitute father figure he could not relate to. For the first time in his life this sad little ten-year-old had found someone who could satisfy his craving to have first priority on someone's time and attention.

Big Brothers do not always work by themselves, nor do all local organizations follow the same pattern. In Michigan, over forty elderly men, members of a senior citizen's group in three different towns, annually contribute hundreds of hours toward the preparation and successful completion of the Big Brothers "Sugarbush" operation each spring. For five days a week men in the grandfather age category are on hand to gather sap, make maple syrup, cook and serve pancakes and sausages to all the Big Brothers, their Little Brothers, and to their families. A good time is had by all.

For information about what you can do where you are, inquire either of your local Big Brothers organization, or write

Big Brothers of America
341 Suburban Station Building
Philadelphia, Pennsylvania 19103

The foregoing are merely representative, not all-inclusive, of the many national organizations that have come around to the point of view that there are many older persons willing to give volunteer service when there is a real need, if they are enabled to do it. Any Chamber of Commerce, voluntary service bureau, or an accommodating librarian will be glad to furnish you with a list of national organizations that have local affiliates in your area. In addition, there are two national organizations whose sole purpose is to engage in activities that enhance the chances for independence, dignity, and purpose of men and women in the upper age brackets. No one who assents to the idea that these three factors are the essentials of a well-rounded life at any age should fail to get acquainted with them.

American Association of Retired Persons

The American Association of Retired Persons, open to anybody past his fifty-fifth birthday, was founded in 1958. Its sister organization, the National Retired Teachers Association, was organized eleven years earlier. Together they now have over a million and a half members. Their late founder, Dr. Ethel Andrus, dynamic even in her eighties, used to say that "creative energy is ageless." It was her firm conviction, which forms today the basis of both organization's programs, that "years of experience, understanding and skill are reserves of energy and power that must be put to work."

Both organizations aim to help members build richer, more interesting lives. Anyone who wants to find fellowship and pursue common interests, and at the same time make a contribution to society, can attain his ends by joining one of the nearly thirteen hundred local units of the two organizations.

Both offer various kinds of insurance and health programs, adult education courses, consumer forums, and diverse choices of group travel. In addition, most chapters engage in a wide variety of projects dictated largely by local needs. Individual members are spurred on to become active in legislation, sometimes act as consultants in their fields to governmental or nonprofit organizations, or operate thrift shops with fellow members, etc. The following are representative activities launched locally.

The South Nassau County, New York AARP Chapter furnished volunteers to New York's State Employment service. Their special function was to assist the professional staff in finding jobs for older men and women.

In Santa Barbara, California, the chapter operates a daily reassurance telephone service for the benefit of the homebound.

Retired teachers through their chapter in Grand Rapids, Michigan, participated in a tutorial program in low income areas under sponsorship of the Urban League, the Parent-Teacher Association, and a local high school whose students were predominantly black.

In the same state, in Saginaw, a project for aid to delinquent boys and girls was carried on in cooperation with the Juvenile Court. It was so successful that subsequently funds were appropriated by the county for an educational program and eventually the construction of a modern building to house it.

For information, and the address of the chapter nearest you, write

National Retired Teachers Association (over 1100 chapters)
or

American Association of Retired Persons (there are over 600 chapters)

Western Headquarters: 215 Long Beach Blvd.,
Times Building, Long Beach, Calif. 90802

Eastern Headquarters:
1225 Connecticut Avenue, N.W.,
Washington, D.C. 20036

The National Council of Senior Citizens

Another powerful and stimulating organization to belong to is the National Council of Senior Citizens, which claims two million members. It has been in the forefront of every legislative struggle in the last decades to secure at least minimum comfort and a decent income for every person who reaches late years without them. For instance, the National Council of Senior Citizens is credited in having a large share in the long-drawn-out struggle that eventually brought about Medicare, through weight of much testimony at Congressional hearings and the loyal backing of its membership. Others of its long-time goals include achievement of good low-cost housing for the elderly poor, jobs for those who need them in their declining years, and property tax relief for aged home owners on limited incomes.

However, you do not have to have a special interest in one of its projects to become both a useful member and to gain something from the membership for yourself. The approximately two thousand clubs affiliated with the Council throughout the United States work as local units to encourage intelligent political discussions, act as consultants to community organizations or enroll as their volunteers. In general their purpose is to create a better society for all Americans.

Like the AARP and the NRTA, the National Council of Senior Citizens offers individual benefits for members. It, too, offers a nonprofit drug service, life insurance, and low-cost travel plans. Its main purpose, however, is to give support to legislation aimed at assisting older persons to lead useful lives in independence.

For literature, information, and a list of affiliates, write

National Council of Senior Citizens, Inc.
1627 E Street, N.W., Washington, D.C. 20006

The Outlook

Most agencies with a national scope today pay at least lip service to the dictum found in Job 12:12 (RSV): "Wisdom is with the aged, and understanding in length of days." There is no question about your finding more than one that will regard your experience as an asset. There is an exhilaration in becoming part of any program; no one can feel forlorn or isolated, even if he is bedbound, when he has a part, however humble, in helping a good cause progress. But when you are a cog in national machinery that has impact on the lives of people you may never see, and when you take this action because you have realized that retirement is neither the end nor the beginning, but is a normal state of life which simply requires a change in emphasis, you can really make your contribution count.

Chapter VII

Volunteering Under Government Auspices

Long before the first White House Conference on Aging called attention in 1961 to the fact that people were not only living longer but retaining their vigor into old age, certain governmental organizations had already found out those facts and made use of them. For more than a quarter-century a number had been putting to good use capacities of older adults. Many hundreds of thousands of people in their sixties, seventies, and eighties today work without salary and without fanfare within the framework of great Federal agencies that deeply touch the hearts and lives of all Americans.

The U.S. government makes a conscious effort to set an example to the private sector in its employment practices, and does the same in its use of human resources on a volunteer basis. Age is not a barrier, if other qualifications are present, to any man or woman who wants to express love of humanity in work that is not paid for in dollars.

If you join the volunteer staff of an agency that extends its work to your own community you will be helping your fellow citizens in it just as much as you would if you did work for a local philanthropy. There are so many Federal organizations, and their work is so

134

divergent, you have a wide choice. The following are some typical examples.

Veterans Administration Voluntary Service

The Veterans Administration's Voluntary Service (commonly known as VAVS) is so vast and so outstanding, and so necessary, that there are ample opportunities to become part of its broad network of services, in and out of hospitals.

Since the end of World War II the VAVS has enrolled volunteers of all ages, depending on the capability of the individual to do a particular piece of work. Some older people fulfill assignments that younger ones cannot do as well, and vice versa.

"Growing old is in many instances a question of an attitude of mind. It does not necessarily follow you must fold your hands and rest."

These are not a couple of platitudes. They represent the consensus of researches into the psychology of aging at the Veterans Administration Hospital in Houston, Texas, one of thirty-eight that conduct research into the aging process. But equally important, the statements represent the attitude of the administrative staff in the one hundred and sixty-seven Veterans Administration Hospitals, its fifty-nine regional offices, its numerous outpatient clinics, its domiciliaries and nursing home care units—in short it is an attitude that insures your welcome.

The Veterans Administration does not keep statistics indicating the birth date of its volunteers; nevertheless, it is known that at some of its hospitals and other facilities at least half of the volunteers were born before 1900, all of them performing worthwhile services.

WHY VOLUNTEERS ARE NEEDED

Since the end of World War II, Veterans Administration hospitals have been enormously improved. Today they are considered among our leading medical care services. Since they are staffed and financed by the government, you might well ask why each year an average of some 108,000 men and women (many over sixty-five and a few past eighty) are needed as volunteers.

It is true that the Veterans Administration operates the largest network of hospitals, out-patient clinics, day treatment centers, rehabilitation and nursing home care units in the United States. It is also true it has a large paid staff for all of them. But the Administration's medical authorities find that professional staff, no matter how capable, cannot do what staff and volunteers working together can do. The latter can help both in getting patients well and in lightening the burdens of illness or disability, temporary or permanent. The regular staff, however conscientious, cannot fill all the moments in a seriously disabled patient's life; perhaps when gloomy thoughts set in, volunteers can, if there are enough of them. It has been proved without question that through personal visits, reading aloud, talking when necessary in a patient's mother tongue if he was not born here, entertaining a group, teaching, counseling, helping with hobbies—and more—volunteers can do much to displace worries and dispel loneliness. For the bedfast patient with a long-term disability the volunteer may be as important as his nurse, and when he returns home, perhaps even more.

WHAT YOU CAN DO

There is so much that is unique in the Veterans Administration's Voluntary Service everybody ought to be able to find his own place. The facilities themselves are widely varied. There are hospitals primarily for patients who need general medical attention or surgery; some exist mainly to give psychiatric care. There are also institutions that must serve for at least a semi-permanent and sometimes a permanent home for those whose disabilities prevent their living in the community of their own choosing. And there are also clinics for those who need to come only for out-patient treatment.

Because the facilities are so varied, the assignments can be. Men are as necessary as women volunteers. Through letter-writing or a dozen other kinds of personal services, all do many things a patient cannot do for himself. In what has been termed "the largest organization of volunteers in the world," compassionate men and women are teaching radio and television repair and hook-rug weaving; wheeling patients to look and listen to entertainments; helping them

136

to cultivate such hobbies as horticulture, photography, carpentry; and finding other ways to lighten the burden of long days.

The list at the Veterans Administration Hospital in New York is typical; so is the fact that in any average year elderly men and women make up about 20 percent of the total number of volunteers. They conduct bingo games; show motion pictures; aid in occupational therapy, help out in office tasks, in the library; and so on. Generally speaking, you can make a choice everywhere in these fields:

Recreation: The purpose is to develop interpersonal relations.

Resocialization activities: Such as parties and ward entertainments.

Sports: These are as varied as the patients and the volunteers.

Patient care: Including feeding, escort services, reading, writing.

Library work: Acting as ward cart assistant, or assistant in library or clerical work, and so on.

Chaplain service: Ushers, musicians, escorts, and so forth.

Occupational therapy: Arts, crafts, manual arts, painting, music teaching, demonstrating.

There is also a perpetual need for discussion leaders, editors for hospital newspapers, exhibitors to arrange stamp or other hobby shows, aids for the dietetic or housekeeping services, the social work department, and so on. In every one of these miscellaneous jobs, and in all others, the volunteer supplements, but does not substitute for the staff member.

This graphic picture of one long-time volunteer at the eighteen-hundred-bed psychiatric hospital in Montrose, New York, tells much to any older person. This is how the Director of Voluntary service pictured her:

She comes twice a week . . . visits and feeds the helpless neurological patients. She is one of the few volunteers who spends time with the tuberculosis patients. She assists with a special Protestant religious

137

service once a week. She teaches Braille to two blind patients. She has found a new life for herself during her years as a volunteer. She's hale, hearty, walks an average of seven miles during her volunteer day —and she's *eighty-six*.

MORE VOLUNTEERS ARE NEEDED

In spite of the fact that considerably over a hundred thousand volunteers in an average year give more than eight and a half million hours in reclaiming human lives, the Veterans Administration can use more. As far ahead as anyone can see, as a result of the Vietnam war and other embroilments, and the backwash of those in the past, the number of hospitalized veterans will be increasing yearly. In 1957 a half-million were admitted; only ten years later there were many times that number. Those who were already institutionalized as a result of two world wars are getting older; they are the ones who often particularly welcome older callers. However adequately our government provides for these diverse groups there will remain needs that only volunteers, free from governmental regulations and limitations, can meet.

If you shun the idea of helping out in a medical institution, you might be able to become part of the program that helps the patient in the first stages, or later if he needs it, when he returns to life in the community. This is how it works:

When patients still under the VA's care are placed in communities at some distance from the hospital, follow-up services are sometimes provided by a traveling social worker. When voluntary assistance is needed, the hospital directs a request for help to organized community groups interested in providing aid to men (and women, too) trying to make adjustments to life outside a hospital regime. These are some of the ways patients are aided by volunteers coming to their homes:

1. Friendly visiting (to bring contacts with the outside)
2. Giving aid in homemaker services
3. Helping with "meals on wheels" or with meal preparation
4. Taking patients to social events, to church, to the doctor
5. Helping to develop a hobby interest

6. Doing actual housework or making minor repairs
7. Staying with patient to relieve the family for a short while
8. Arranging, or assisting, with installation of rails, ramps, and so on

In short, the range is anything from giving physical aid in tasks as yet too strenuous, to helping a man ready for a job to find one, or tactfully assisting him through the difficult period of learning again such normal activities as joining an organization. One of the most useful jobs anybody can do for a returned veterans' program of this kind is simply to offer knowledge of the community and its resources and know what they are prepared to do to help a man struggling to get back to independent life.

There are two ways to offer your services, even if you have only a few hours of time each week to invest. The first is to get in touch with the Director of Voluntary Service at the nearest Veterans Administration Hospital and discuss what there is to do and what part you can play in it. (See Appendix.)

The second way is to be a member of a community organization that has chosen to participate in a project approved by the Veterans hospital. There are many of these, and they are not necessarily limited to patriotic activities. If you already belong to an organization and think its members might join in sponsoring some work on behalf of veterans, the place to talk it over is at the Veterans Hospital. They are located in every state of the Union, except Alaska and Hawaii (where veterans are cared for, too, but in other Federal hospitals), in Puerto Rico, and in the District of Columbia.

There are two pamphlets that will tell you all you need to know in advance of your participation:

You as a Volunteer
Veterans Administration
Pamphlet, 10-46

The Patient Returns to the Community
Veterans Administration Pamphlet 18-83

Both can be procured from the nearest Veterans Administration Hospital, without charge.

Red Cross, a Quasi-governmental Organization

The American National Red Cross is only one of approximately forty other national organizations that furnish volunteers to every kind of facility maintained by the Veterans Administration, but in the public mind the Red Cross—to use its familiar abbreviation—is different. Although, strictly speaking, it is not a governmental organization and there is neither a direct governmental connection nor support from government funds, it is chartered by Congerss. Its obligation to provide volunteer services to veterans is embodied in the responsibility outlined in the charter "to furnish voluntary aid to sick and wounded personnel of the armed forces." And this also includes its vast overseas program.

For retirees and those who are looking forward to what they will do when working hours are cut down or cease, the Red Cross has a special significance. Like the Veterans Administration, the American National Red Cross has made a special effort to enlist the aid of men and women who, because they have retired from business, a profession, or other full-time responsibilities, can give more time than those still at work. As long ago as 1953, all age ceilings were removed from volunteer posts by the Red Cross. The effect of this official step was felt not only within the approximately 3,300 chapters that crisscross the United States, but in the entire field of health and welfare organizations. For the public announcement was hailed by educators and professional people working in the old age field as a step forward which should influence the policies and practices of other nonprofit organizations.

How far that influence has been felt is not measurable, but within the Red Cross itself age is not a criterion in either the receipt or the gift of services. People of all ages provide its power and its finances. The cooperation that older men and women can give was once summed up by E. Roland Harriman, National Chairman (himself one of the Red Cross's two million volunteers), in these words:

> The retiree is vital to all our service organizations as our population expands and our needs increase. But this is especially true for the Red Cross since volunteers are its keystone. Millions are needed to carry out its program for the armed services and veterans, its blood donation

program, water safety, first aid, nursing, Junior Red Cross and other community services.

More and more the Red Cross looks to retirees as a source to fill its volunteer gap. They have more maturity and a greater sense of responsibility. And they have warmth, growing out of long experience in human relationships.

To lend credence to these glowing words, glance at these random examples of men and women who have found great satisfaction in what they do. None of them think of themselves as unusual (nor does the American National Red Cross).

Frank C. is a former safety supervisor for a North Carolina utility company. On his thirtieth anniversary as an instructor in first aid and water safety, he received a special award. He remarked, "I should be giving the Red Cross the award for giving me the opportunity to teach. I think I've benefitted more than my pupils."

Jack B., who belongs to a California chapter, helped distribute American Red Cross clothing, food, and medicine in Siberia during World War I. After his retirement he became a volunteer in social welfare aid, a translator and a Gray Man. He explained his multiple activities in these words: "I never forgot the gratitude of those desperate people in Siberia and vowed one day I would serve the Red Cross. When I retired from business I began to do it and was busier—and happier— than before."

There is room even for the willing person who is bedbound. In one Eastern community there is an eighty-year-old woman who has twice been co-chairman of a financial campaign for the Red Cross chapter in her area, in spite of the fact that for years she has been unable to leave her home. Nobody has ever told her she is unable mentally, physically, or chronologically to carry out her duties. By lively, constant use of her telephone each year she produces considerable results.

"Red Cross volunteers are of all ages, all occupations . . . and perform all kinds of useful service." This is how an advertisement in New York City papers began. Whether you live in a great metropolis

141

like this or in a small town, the list of possibilities for those who have a few hours a week or more to spare, by and large, falls into the same categories:

Hospitals: Volunteers (who used to be known as "Gray Ladies" and "Gray Men" and in a few communities still are) are useful not only in military and veterans' hospitals, but in county, mental, and children's hospitals, and in sanitariums, rehabilitation centers, and in nursing homes.

Instruction: This covers a wide gamut, ranging from teaching first aid, water safety, home nursing, mother and baby care, to fly-tying, and tutoring for the underprivileged.

Transportation: A corps of people who can drive cars to get old and young out of homes, hospitals, and other static situations is a need everywhere.

Office work: Under this undramatic term, one can do publicity, fundraising, accounting, and anything else that makes an office run well.

Disasters: In the public mind, the Red Cross is intimately and dramatically associated with rescue work necessitated by overflowing waters, earthquakes, tornadoes, and other awesome outbreaks from natural and unnatural causes. In all of them there is ample room for volunteer help to provide food, shelter, transportation, baby and other care on a person-to-person basis.

Armed forces: There is practically no aid omitted; the range is from letter-writing and reading for blinded military men to instruction in hobbies, bedside home nursing, to just plain visiting to dispel loneliness and give comfort.

Two examples suffice to indicate that a choice of activities is as wide as one's interests and personal abilities.

Mrs. Bess Sandford Lee of Mitchell, Nebraska, was eighty years old in December, 1967. The patients at the Western Nebraska Nursing Home gave her a birthday party. Mrs. Lee, a pioneer rancher's widow, had logged nearly five hundred hours in weekly visits to the

142

home over a period of six years. As a representative of the North Platte Valley Chapter, she read to and visited with residents, wrote letters for them, and did their shopping. She exemplifies the best qualities of a Red Cross volunteer, her birthday party-givers said— faithfulness and sincerity.

At the other end of the country, George C. O'Brien was recruited by the Red Cross Chapter in Westchester County, north of New York City. Mr. O'Brien drove sixty miles twice a week to a Veterans Administration psychiatric hospital. He helped patients about to be discharged to prepare themselves to look for and secure jobs. One of Mr. O'Brien's most sought-after courses was called "Selling Yourself to Industry." It was a duplicate of what he had taught young people for years at a New York college. After years of working for large corporations, Mr. O'Brien had retired. Of his experiences at the veterans' hospital Mr. O'Brien said, "This is the best job I ever had!"

You do not have to be highly skilled to be a good Red Cross volunteer, though there are training courses you can take if you wish. Many jobs involve no more than warmth of feeling and a sense of responsibility toward the job and toward your neighbor. Nobody illustrates this more than members of a Golden Age Center in Cleveland who volunteered to help semi-helpless elderly patients in a Veterans Administration hospital eat their evening meal.

The volunteers had a short orientation course and Red Cross home nursing training lessons before they began. The two hours they spent at the hospital one or two days a week often entailed postponing their own dinners. Sometimes forty-five minutes were needed to feed just one almost helpless man. But Mrs. Ella Hicks, one of the volunteers, voiced what everyone felt from the outset. She said, "I don't know when I've felt more useful. I really get a lift from the cheerfulness of a man who has been bedridden five years and yet can say when you ask him how he is, 'I'm O.K.!' "

To seek out your own milieu get in touch with the local Red Cross chapter; it will be listed in the telephone book under that or the formal name of the organization. If you want more information or literature, address

Office of Volunteers, National Headquarters
The American National Red Cross
Washington, D.C. 20006

The SCORE Program

If your bent leads you away from the sick or the disabled, if you prefer to work with adults who are carrying on their everyday affairs, if you want to give them counseling based on your own business or technical experience, you have a chance to join a group of individuals (of both sexes) who are members of SCORE. The initials stand for Service Corps of Retired Executives, and it is a voluntary arm of the Small Business Administration of our Federal government.

The basic purpose of SCORE is to help businesses and small plants that need managerial or technical assistance. SCORE was the bold, imaginative answer to two problems about which the government was, and is, deeply concerned. The first is the high rate of small business failures. There are, on the average, about thirteen thousand such debacles every year. This is bad not only for the owners but for our country. It is a proved, indisputable fact that most of them fail largely because of the ignorance and mismanagement of their owners, all well-meaning individuals trying to carry on the American ideal of independence, but with insufficient management knowledge —or capital—to do it successfully.

The second problem with which the Small Business Administration concerns itself is the potentially large-scale waste of talents of retired executives who have had their own businesses or who have held responsible jobs.

SCORE was established in 1964 to combat both business failures and the failure of our country to use the skills of the retired executive as fully as possible. Within six months after the program was launched more than a thousand retired businessmen had volunteered to help, and more than five thousand small business owners had asked their aid. The program was first tested over a period of months in Boston and Washington, D.C. Three years after that the two hundred and second chapter was launched in Puerto Rico, and over three thousand SCORE volunteers were on the national roster.

144

By that time over 40,000 businesses and small plants (each with less than twenty-five employees) had been given free assistance. A small grocery store owner in a Chicago slum district was one of them, his story represents the kind of work, except for its details, that you will be doing if you join this effort at harnessing national talents.

One day a scrap of paper was handed around to twenty volunteers assembled for their regular monthly meeting at the Chicago headquarters of the Small Business Administration. On the paper was plaintively scrawled, "Can you send someone to show me how to make money?"

SCORE volunteers are always assigned on the basis of their familiarity with the problems of a particular business. William A. Cassin was the volunteer selected that day because, before he joined SCORE, he was President of the Central Grocers Cooperative, Inc. When he called and introduced himself, he found his discouraged client totting up the day's proceeds in a dingy back room. Mr. Cassin asked for the last financial statement. The answer he received would be only too familiar to other SCORE members. "What's a financial statement?" the would-be successful grocer asked.

SCORE volunteers are not expected to do a client's work for him; their role is to teach him how to do it himself. Mr. Cassin began by patiently unraveling what he could through the grocer's hazy memory of financial transactions. Afterwards, he advised the man to take advantage of a simple bookkeeping course the Small Business Administration was offering. The grocer took not one, but two courses, and under SCORE'S tutelage learned that he does not always have to be skirting disaster. At last report, he was well established in a small way, and doing what he wanted to do in the beginning—making money.

Have you had experience in marketing, sales, advertising, finance, personnel relations, production, control, engineering, or any other phase of industry? If so, SCORE can use you to help the businessman in your own area who is in trouble. You will spend as much time as necessary, when you are assigned, to uncover and diagnose the cause of difficulties; then, like a physician, you will give a prescription for them.

If you want to join this heterogeneous group of retired people you will have to have, as they have, the ability to explain both the short-comings of your clients and the remedies you are recommending in terms that the inexperienced can understand. You will be in good company. For former corporate treasurers; comptrollers; production or sales managers; exentrepreneurs; others with experience in accountancy, law, or income tax—all part of the vast and variegated pool of business knowledge in the United States—will be your fellow members. At your monthly meetings, you will be associating with men and women with experience in production, wholesaling, retailing, banking, transportation, foreign trade—the whole gamut of the business structure that makes our nation the most powerful in the world.

Your counseling is free to the client, but you will be entitled to modest traveling expenses ($5.00 within a twenty-five mile radius). If you are like the majority of your co-volunteers you will not ask for even that. Your satisfaction, like theirs, and your reward, will be in the completion of a task well done.

Easy cases will require only a few hours of your time. On the other hand some SCORE counselors like what they are doing so well they do not count the time they spend on it in any sense wasted. One retired Washington attorney ministered for months to a truck sales and repair shop that grossed a half-million dollars and yet was losing $5,000 a year. Today this once-floundering enterprise makes a five-figure profit—because of SCORE.

The Small Business Administration does not consider its volunteers philanthropists, and neither does it expect them to be social workers. They are hardheaded realists who believe profoundly in the future of our country and the necessity to help those often tiny business concerns at the bottom who have a basic advantage over big business because they have a personalized relationship with their customers. On the other hand these businesses need help because they sometimes lack both the imagination and the know-how to capitalize on their great assets.

The effect on both the giver of advice and the one to whom it is given can be dynamic. "It makes me feel twenty years younger," says a retired retailer in the Midwest. "You have no idea what a thrill there is in helping somebody prosper and knowing you're responsible in part for his success!"

This kind of aid is a far cry from the dole or the breadline. It is in the line of the best American tradition of helping people learn how to help themselves. If you want to be a member of SCORE, write or telephone the nearest Small Business Administration Office. (See Appendix for list of Regional offices.) You will be supplied with the name and address of the person at the head of the nearest chapter. If you are living in the country or in a tiny village, you still can be a part of SCORE when the occasion arises for your aid. For information, write

> Service Corps of Retired Executives
> Small Business Administration
> 1441 L Street, N.W.
> Washington, D.C. 20416

Anti-Poverty Programs

The national war against poverty is likely to last for years to come, but whether some or all of the projects launched by the Economic Opportunity Act and its various amendments will continue to be Federally financed is a matter of year-to-year decision. Nevertheless, the imprint they have made is already indelible and for an older generation is already bearing fruit. For the first time in our entire history, the worth and value of older people to the upbuilding of the United States, even when they have no considerable bank accounts on which to draw, has been officially recognized in our national planning. Because the successes of some of these projects have helped many older people rise above the poverty level, prejudices have been broken down. That will make it easier for all older people to be accepted elsewhere, whether or not being paid for what they do is of any moment to them.

For the impact of a presidential statement such as the following was not lost on privately supported organizations. Former President Johnson, in a message dealing with anti-poverty programs, included this in his statements:

The most enduring strength of our nation is the huge reservoir of talent, initiative and leadership which exists at every level of our society. . . . Among older people who have retired there are many Americans who are ready to enlist in our war against poverty. They have the skill and the dedication. They are badly needed.

How much of the Federal machinery will finally be retained, or taken over by states or municipalities in which the projects have been successful; whether or not the federal pattern will be repeated everywhere, followed at all, or expanded, are things that each year can change, according to the Administration's policies and Congressional appropriations. (The first steps toward transferring some anti-poverty programs to local control was launched through amendments passed in 1967.) Whatever happens, there are still many ways that you can become part of the tremendous national effort to overcome hardships of those who still live below the poverty level. One way to find out what needs to be done is to examine a publication first published in 1964 by the Federal Office of Economic Opportunity. Whether or not it is continued, as heretofore, on an annual basis, it will be available as long as supplies last, on request. If it does nothing else, it will show you the immense scope of the opportunities open to you. It contains the statement, *"Volunteers are wanted, aged eighteen to eighty-five."* The publication's sole purpose is to give accurate, detailed information to persons in all parts of the country willing and able to donate services needed in what has been loosely termed "our war on poverty." Send for latest edition of

Voluntary Help Wanted
Information Center
Office of Economic Opportunity
Room 212, Washington, D.C. 20506 (free)

THE OBJECTIVES OF THE ANTI-POVERTY PROGRAM

In its third edition in 1967 the publication pointed out, "There are hundreds of thousands of anonymous Americans who have given volunteer help to the anti-poverty programs." They were (and are) doing it for preschool children, for neighborhood educational and recreational programs in their own communities, or coaching or even

148

offering overnight or weekend hospitality to young Job Corps enrollees trying to climb out of unemployability.

There have been mistakes made, but no one can doubt that government-sponsored projects like this deserve volunteer support. They have also restored dignity and a sense of usefulness to many thousands of older people, eager as they are to be a vital part of the national scene. William Perry Morrison expressed this attitude in telling terms.

Mr. Morrison is one of the workers in "Green Thumbs," which has been called "America's most beautiful anti-poverty program." It was launched in a number of states both to conserve and enhance the appearance of our parks, highways, and town squares, and to give employment to older Americans who can do the work. Though it pays only a minimum wage, Mr. Morrison is one of many who see something more than money that they gain from it. To an inquiring reporter who watched him planting with loving care, he said, "Green Thumbs is just like a man getting married and having his children carry on. By the same token us Green Thumbers create something for coming generations to enjoy and remember us by!"

Like all initial attempts at drastic change, many of the new ideas and the way they were implemented have been faulty; they have been criticized often, sometimes severely. Nevertheless, at the least, the publicity given to conditions that had often been glossed over or ignored has made a deep dent in national apathy. Regardless of what political wave sweeps over the country, the gaps between the haves and the have-nots can never again be completely overlooked. You will have ample chances to help wipe them out because in some form or another, some of the programs that have been successful will be continued and should be reaching out for your help. The following are typical, not all-inclusive, and have made excellent use of the strengths of the older Americans and their ability to help not only themselves, but others worse off.

FOSTER GRANDPARENT PROGRAM

Of all the anti-poverty programs, this is probably the most appealing. Its success has not only brightened the lives of many institutionalized children, but the favorable impact made by this unique effort, aptly named, will make it easier hereafter for you and every other older person who wants to bridge the generation gap, to cross it.

The Foster Grandparent program has amply proved that those without professional training, and even without much schooling, can favorably affect the lives of boys and girls in orphanages and other institutions by simply following the prescription of giving them individualized "tender, loving care." The same prescription has a good chance of success with neglected or forlorn children in any environment.

The Federal program was launched by the Office of Economic Opportunity in 1965 and supervised by the Administration on Aging. Under the plan nobody earning more than $1,500 annually could be hired. Just two years after it began there were already forty-seven programs in full swing at one hundred institutions in thirty-three states and Puerto Rico. Nearly three thousand men and women, all over sixty, many in their seventies, and a few in their eighties, were spending two hours a day five days a week with each of two children. They were not hired to give physical, medical, or nursing care. They were offering what physicians prescribe for the forlorn of any age— attention to emotional needs. They were also proving that an effective substitute for the old-time family relationship between grandparents and the offspring of their children can be translated into effective terms even within the walls of an institution. They were helping boys and girls not related to them by blood ties to become something other than emotional cripples as adults.

For many older men and women the needed supplement to their income was not the only favorable factor. As one sprightly grandmother said, "It's wonderful! I'm not on the shelf anymore—this program has opened up a whole new world to me!"

After its first successes of the beginning years, the program spread annually to more institutions in more states; the doors opened to older people, you may be sure, will never be completely closed again.

At one children's home the director said, "Kids are walking, kids are talking, kids who used to have to be tranquilized aren't being tranquilized with drugs any more. Kids who couldn't go to school, go to school now. For the first time in their lives, they've got someone all their own; it makes all the difference in the world."

If this seems professional extravagance, touching evidence that it is true can be found in a letter from an institutionalized little girl in the Midwest. She wrote about Foster Grandparents:

> A grandfather is a man grandmother. He goes for walks with the boys and they talk about fishing and things like that. . . .
> Grandmas don't have to do anything except be there. . . . It is better for us if they don't typewrite or play cards, except with us. They don't have to be smart, only answer questions like why dogs hate cats and how come God isn't married. They don't talk baby talk like visitors do, because it is hard to understand. When they read to us, they don't skip words or mind if it is the same story again.
> Everybody should try to have a grandmother . . . because grandmas are the only grownups who have got time. . . .

Who can measure exactly how much an older person receives from this kind of relationship?

If the idea of giving individualized attention to neglected or handicapped children appeals to you, you do not have to be formally enrolled as a foster grandparent to do the work; that much publicly praised program will be known wherever you apply. If you are willing to be supervised by a professionally trained person, if you have both understanding of and interest in the needs of unfortunate children, apply to any institution that they have to call "home." Staffs everywhere, however good-hearted, are inevitably too few in numbers and too occupied with vital duties to give the personal interest that a volunteer can offer. Men as well as women are needed, as one director put it, "to become the familiar friend which the too busy staff member can't be." The projects may be federally supported. However, governmental programs also change from time to time, and even their names alter with their budgets. The success of the Foster Grandparent program has stimulated new programs locally, sometimes on a statewide basis, to enrich the lives of boys and girls not always institutionalized and not always poor.

For an up-to-date view of the national picture and how you may be able to fit into it where you live, write the nearest

Regional Office,
Office of Economic Opportunity (see Appendix)

or

Foster Grandparent Program
Administration on Aging
Washington, D.C. 20201

VISTA *(Volunteers in Service to America)*

Another one of the Office of Economic Opportunity programs likely to endure in one form or another has had an especial appeal to retirees and has made a special effort to enroll them. It is known as VISTA (Volunteers in Service to America), and is often called the "domestic Peace Corps."

"If you want to serve your nation in a vital role, if you like to help people help themselves, if you have the patience, courage, and the will to accept a challenging assignment, then VISTA may be your answer to an active retirement."

This is the message over the signature of Sargent Shriver, former head of the Office of Economic Opportunity, in a leaflet aimed specifically at attracting retired people. Its significant title is "At My Age?" (You can get a copy by writing the nearest OEO regional office. See Appendix.)

VISTA volunteers are people old and young, willing to give a year of their lives, or re-enroll for two or three, to work in the deep South among minority groups, on Indian reservations, in migrant worker camps, in rural villages, or in large cities. They go where they are needed, and they work because they share the belief of Dr. Samuel H. Lerner, a retired dentist, who was accepted when he was seventy-two. He applied, he said, because "our society can and should offer help to every individual so he can work out his personal or social problems to the best of his ability."

The following random list will tell you that whatever career you may have had, it can be used. You can forget how old you are. To date, at eighty-six, Edgar Slater is VISTA'S oldest volunteer. After careers in both engineering and teaching, Mr. Slater worked two years with the Crow Indians of Montana. He taught blueprint reading and

152

construction techniques so well several of his Indian friends were able to build their own homes. During his final six months he designed equipment for a Head Start class of preschool boys and girls on the reservation. Then he asked VISTA if he could do another job somewhere! Less spectacularly, from the point of view of years, retirees are working individually and in couples all over the country. Mrs. Jay Morgan is only sixty-five; her husband sixty-eight. Together they left their Michigan home to work among California's migrant farm workers, and organized day care and educational centers for the migrants' children. The gamut elsewhere runs something like this:

Homemakers are teaching cooking, sewing, home management. They are helping mothers learn how to care for their babies and toddlers; they are aiding ex-rural families to adjust to city life.

Teachers have organized both day schools and remedial programs. They teach foreign-born adults how to read and write English, counsel school dropouts, and do tutoring of both children and their parents.

Businessmen provide counseling to small entrepreneurs like the volunteers of SCORE, but those in VISTA live among the people they counsel. They help jobless young people learn how to apply for and hold jobs they get. They tell unsuccessful business people what they ought to know about Federal, state, or other aid, and how and when and where to apply for loans if needed.

Farmers help small independent owners of acreage or tenant farmers adopt better methods to meet competition. They assist their clients to get loans or other forms of assistance and sometimes show members of their families how to earn extra income, and give counseling on everything that affects the lives of those on the land.

Nurses and medical technicians of various kinds promote hygiene and sanitation, organize clinics, and teach baby and child care.

Attorneys. Assisting individuals is only one side of their work. They help both people and organizations, interpreting the law and aiding them to secure the right kind of legal help when they need it.

There are also carpenters, plumbers, industrial workers, engineers, accountants, salesmen, office workers, and managers—each with something to contribute.

Are you too interested in changing the world around you? Do you refuse to become resigned to the pockets of poverty and help-lessness that still shame our rich nation?

If the answer is "yes" to both questions, VISTA will welcome your help in aiding people to move out of the poverty cycle. The mere fact that you will be living among the people with whom you work is a factor in earning their trust and respect. You will never be sent to a community where you are not wanted. The official atti-tude always has been that "volunteers are sent on request, given specific jobs to do, and enough freedom to be creative and effective." Specifically, these are the regulations:

1. Volunteers serve for one year and work under supervision of state and local anti-poverty agencies that have requested their service.

2. They receive a monthly stipend of $50, which is set aside for them until they complete their service.

3. All living allowances are paid, but geared to the standards of the area in which they serve.

4. Volunteers receive intensive training for a period of weeks accord-ing to the specific type of project (urban, Indian, migrant). The training is given by leading universities, social service organizations, and so forth. Trainees perform on-the-job assignments similar to those they will eventually do.

5. Selection is based on such qualities as emotional stability, maturity, of attitude, dependability, motivation.

6. If a married couple applies, both husband and wife must qualify.

The Ernest Martinsons—he, a seventy-year-old retired civil en-gineer and building contractor, his wife sixty-nine—did qualify. To-gether they went to Boone County, West Virginia, along the Little Coal River where times are generally hard. In just one year they helped renovate more than thirty wretched homes.

If you would like to look at a questionnaire that will help you identify your own likes, dislikes, preferences, and the assets that can assist people outside your own community, write for information and an application blank to

Liaison, Programs for Older Workers
Volunteers in Service to America
Office of Economic Opportunity
Washington, D.C. 20506

Even if you cannot leave home, or do not want to, there is another angle to VISTA's work which can use you. Its Citizen Corps complements the work its VISTA volunteers do in a community. You can work with them a few hours or a few days a week, for improvement of your community's school system, town council, courts, multiple-purpose centers, or any other community action program trying to identify and meet needs where you live. Whether you are a housewife without business training, or a business or professional man or woman with long years of experience behind you, you can apply at the regional office of VISTA. (See Appendix.) You will not receive any stipend, and no part of your living expenses will be covered because you are working out of affection for the place you call home.

Lessons from the Job Corps Program

The Job Corps program has been probably the most hotly debated of all the projects launched by the Office of Economic Opportunity, but whether it survives in any form at all, it carries some elements that ought not to be lost on any older person because it often dramatized what they can do.

The Job Corps was intended as a national residential training program located in various parts of the United States. It was conceived to help young women and men out of school and out of work prepare to take a place in society. It made excellent use of men and women in the upper age brackets as instructors and counselors. If you are concerned not only by society's ills but by the dissatisfaction that many young people express in violent action, you will be in-

155

terested in the comments that the Director of the Program Development Division of the Job Corps made. In a report sent the heads of each Job Center he said, in part:

"Our Job Corps kids relate well to older people." (The "kids" were in the age range of 14 to 21.)

"Elderly people represent a wealth of talent needed in our Job Corps Centers."

"Elderly people have been a stabilizing influence in our Centers; their rate of turnover is less."

(Note that last remark; it is not lost on any organization carrying on a recruitment campaign that the young volunteer may have more calls on his interests than the older one and be more fickle.) This is just one of many examples of the good reputation older folk built up at Job Centers. At the Trapper Creek Job Center in Montana, Dr. Joseph began at a rather late age an entirely new teaching career. He was a college botany professor who was gladly tutoring young corpsmen on a one-to-one basis in reading and mathematics. His enrollees called this eighty-year-old man "Joe." He got along well with them not because he speaks four languages (several of them prevalent among the Corpsmen) but because he genuinely likes and understands them. His lunch hour was usually spent in playing baseball with them.

This experience is not confined to just one extraordinary man.

At the conservation center in Wellfleet, Massachusetts, located in an area in which many retired professional people live, a number contributed four or more hours a week regularly, both in coaching students and in supervising recreation. One retired engineer gave ten hours weekly just in supervising the center's lapidary shop. Many such teacher-pupil relationships endured long after the corpsmen, when trained to hold jobs in industry, left the Center.

Other Government Programs

There is a special challenge in becoming part of a government program. As in any other, the horizon is not limited to volunteering in philanthropic fields, or in raising the economic level of the down-trodden. One example suffices to prove the truth that the number of ways one can be a good citizen are as numerous as the interest of the citizen himself. All that is needed is to have the curiosity—and the industry—to find out where they are.

The United States Weather Bureau is just one of them. It relies on volunteers called "cooperative weather observers" to provide accurate observations regularly from some area where they live. The Bureau is proud of the record made by its older observers, who in some cases have served it for years. They have recorded day-by-day weather in rain, snowstorms, sleet, cold, or at any other time, often when only the hearty like to be out-of-doors. Age of the applicant is not a consideration in reviewing the application, provided it does not affect the quality of work to be done. The criterion applied impartially to both young and old is the ability and willingness to provide faithful recordings of temperature and precipitation.

If you wish to add a bit to the world's knowledge of its environment and become part of a vast weather network, apply to

U.S. Department of Commerce
Environmental Science Services Administration
Weather Bureau, Silver Springs, Maryland 20910

What the Future Can Offer

"Neighborly compassion, voluntarily extended," one graybeard called his own contribution in aiding the federal government to carry out its obligations. It is one of the prime satisfactions of citizenship to be able to employ your greater leisure time and experience in trying to better the world you are going to be a part of—willy-nilly—as long as you live.

In one of his addresses, when he headed the Peace Corps, Sargent Shriver urged older men and women not to be content to lay aside what they had so often painfully learned in life. He said, "It is never too early—or too late—to begin accepting the challenge of our times."

Chapter VIII

Helping the Developing Countries

In every thoughtful discussion of the gap between the have and the have-not nations, the question invariably arises, Where is the supply of experts needed in every field going to come from tomorrow? The delegate from Pakistan at a conference in Puerto Rico, attended by representatives of forty-three developing nations, put it graphically in these words: "It is possible to beg, borrow, and steal money. But it is impossible to beg, borrow, or steal qualified people!"

It is generally believed that this critical situation will exist for years to come. A partial answer to the problem lies in various kinds of work sponsored by business, philanthropic, religious, and governmental organizations in this country, whose impetus spreads around the world. Individually or as a married team, more and more retired people, and some still in mid-career, are using their abilities and sometimes their resources to help out in acute areas overseas. If you share in what one retired executive calls "a glorified vacation with a purpose behind it," you will be joining a constantly increasing stream of physicians, nurses, technicians, secretaries, farmers, teachers, maintenance workers, and housemothers—all people who "care" and do their bit in practical ways. Usually you will find them in areas where age is still regarded with respect and years of experience as a mark of wisdom.

You will not be a missionary in the old-time meaning of the term, but you will be making a contribution to the country in which you are accepted as a temporary resident. You can find organizations that will be glad to enroll you if you are qualified to do their work, either for short-term jobs ranging from three weeks to three months, or for a year or two. If you have a wife and want to take her along, that can be arranged, too; and while she may not formally be enrolled along with you, there will be ample opportunity for her to participate either in using her own special talents or helping you out with yours; or she can use her time to establish an oasis of homelike life overseas. In any case a wife does not have to sit in a foreign country and be bored.

Motivations Vary

If you are curious about the reasons older people are not content to remain for the rest of their lives in their own backyards, however agreeable, and why they are willing to give time and energy in helping people far away, you will find their answers are as varied as the countries they serve in. You will also find that many re-enroll or double the term they agreed on for the reason one retired nurse gave after her West African experience. "It was wonderful!" she wrote. "The remembrance of it will be stimulating for years to come!"

The reason given in more matter-of-fact terms by one man is probably typical of many more. Dr. S. H. Anderman's career goes back to World War II when he served for nearly four years in the armed forces' dental corps. When he was asked his reasons for offering his skills again, this time for a month in a Guatemala hospital where he went with his wife, he answered: "We live in a small town and like to travel and have new experiences. We also like to do useful work and help others less fortunate. This was an opportunity to combine and enjoy both aspirations."

What You Will Gain

There are two questions everybody asks himself.

What will you gain if you go for a short or a long term, without salary, somewhere overseas? Can you really do anything worthwhile in a country that even with foreign assistance and its own development program is barely keeping up with—or perhaps steadily falling behind—its population's needs in good housing, food production, sanitation, control of disease, job training, and employment?

The answer lies in the fact that Americans are working today in almost every nation of the world and in almost every type of job from airline pilot to satellite tracker, from road-builder to agronomist. Those who work for little more than their expenses, or many times pay their own way, testify in letter after letter and to audiences when they come home that they have found it worthwhile to be part of the world scene. Nor does anybody have to be an expert to feel this enthusiasm. Mrs. Adolph R. Klein used smiles, sign language, and music to bridge the gap between herself and the mentally retarded children she worked with in Bangkok while her husband was donating his business knowledge on an assignment in Thailand.

In specific terms, if you apply to some organization and are found to have something that people in some country in Asia, Africa, or South America can benefit by, there are these possibilities:

If you go as an accountant, agriculturist, medical technician, physician, teacher, typist, housemother—or in any other category—you will have opportunities for personal growth that will add a new dimension to your life.

Learning from those whose language or education or political or social customs are different will give you a new insight into the values of American society.

If you are flexible enough, you will be helping to work out emerging social patterns, and if you are inventive enough to go outside of ready-made solutions you may be able to make a positive contribution to your host country.

What Attributes Are Necessary?

Many volunteers of varying ages return to say, "We feel we have received much more than we gave," but if they do, you can be sure that they are the ones who have handled their jobs not only with competence but with love. If you are the kind of person who can keep his eyes open and his spirit free from prejudices you will find beauties in the character and ways of people of another race or another culture. The following self-questions will help you gauge your own potentialities. If you can answer them affirmatively you can be pretty sure that you have the personal qualifications you are going to need, whatever the organization that sends you.

1. Do you have the habit of listening to and learning from others?

2. Do you have a measure of detachment in your personal relations?

3. Do you possess a sense of humor about the inadequacies not only of others but of yourself?

4. Do you possess warmth of personality, and can you communicate your interest in people to them, regardless of how much they differ from you in background?

5. Do you feel you have to do some special kind of work and live in some specific way, or are you willing to take "pot luck" for the sake of the experience and what you can contribute?

No matter what your locale or the trappings of your role (you could be wearing a sweatshirt and dungarees in the jungle, or white tie and tails in the club of an affluent city) you will require stamina. The realistic point of view which Mrs. Allie Sheider Stehr possessed will give you an insight into why she made a success of the job she took.

Mrs. Stehr's husband was a minister; during his lifetime she had been active in several parishes in Illinois; when he died she became a teacher. For the next twenty-seven years Allie Stehr was active either as a teacher or as a school principal. She had long cherished the dream of doing something in overseas service when she retired. But when that time came the teaching posts she first applied for were slow in materializing, so when an urgent call came from Japan she did not hesitate to accept it, especially because Sendai was where one of her three sons had been stationed with the Allied Occupation

Forces, and she felt she already knew what it was like. When she began her work in September, 1965, Mrs. Stehr faced twenty-five English-speaking primary schoolchildren from a variety of backgrounds—ranging from Buddhist to Catholic. All the grades from one to seven were taught by Mrs. Stehr in a setting similar to the one-room schools that used to dot the American landscape.

"A Godsend," "an answer to prayers," and "just the kind of person we wanted," are the ways in which missionaries in the Sendai area spoke of Mrs. Stehr's work.

Mrs. Stehr is a clearheaded woman. She knows that any kind of adjustment in a foreign land requires emotional stability and basic good health. Regarding working in developing areas, Mrs. Stehr says: "I wouldn't recommend it for everybody. A person needs to think twice about going overseas to work after he has reached the age of retirement. No one should accept a post-retirement position abroad if he thinks he is going on a tourist trip. Often the demands on one are greater than when living in the homeland."

But when she is asked if she would recommend at least a temporary teaching post overseas for whoever might want one, she answers with enthusiasm, "Oh, yes! There's nothing like it!"

If you want to know more about her experiences and how she adapted to them, send for a free copy of

The Joy of Post-Retirement Service Overseas. Volunteer Services Commission on Ecumenical Mission and Relations, the United Presbyterian Church in the U.S.A.,
475 Riverside Drive New York, N.Y. 10027

The Responsibility of Our Government

Volunteer efforts not only provide opportunities for interaction among members of different cultures on a person-to-person basis, but they provide occasions for joint action between organizations in our country and those abroad. Both are a concern of the United States; however, many people have a mistaken notion about the responsibility of our government for such programs and their personnel.

If you have any idea of considering an overseas post you ought to know exactly to what extent the United States does interest itself in the work voluntary organizations' personnel do outside its borders.

There is an Advisory Committee on Voluntary Foreign Aid, which is part of the Department of States' Agency for International Development. The Committee was established in 1946, in the wake of the disastrous effects of World War II. It was formed "to tie together the governmental and private programs in the field of foreign relief and to work with interested agencies and groups." That purpose is still relevant. The Committee's purpose is to guide the public, and agencies seeking support of that public, in "appropriate and productive use of contributions for foreign aid." But note this carefully: Neither the Committee, nor the Agency for International Development itself, has any direct jurisdiction over private agencies with overseas programs. However, those who work abroad are usually there with the approval of our own government and the host government.

Registration of voluntary nonprofit agencies with the government's Advisory Committee on Voluntary Foreign Aid is not compulsory. Nevertheless, many do register. There is a safeguard to the public in the fact that the Committee requires those who register with it to report on their income and expenses. About half of the seventy-five agencies that register with the Committee accept—as one benefit of the registration—a subsidy that covers shipment of their own supplies; the host government in turn grants them duty-free entry because those supplies will benefit their nationals. (All the registered agencies have the privilege of briefings, and, if any problems arise in the countries to which their representatives are assigned, the opportunity for consultation and counsel.)

It is a safe generalization to say that most of the important private overseas organizations are going to be registered with the State Department. Although queries about a particular overseas project or the organization that sponsors it should not be put to the Advisory Committee on Voluntary Foreign Aid, there are two things to do to find out what you want to know (in addition to writing directly to the organization itself).

1. The Register of Voluntary Agencies is free to inquirers. Ad-

dress your query to Advisory Committee on Voluntary Foreign Aid, Department of State, Washington, D.C. 20423.

2. There is an American Council of Voluntary Agencies for Foreign Service. As the name implies, this is a membership organization of certain groups with overseas programs. NOTE: The Council does not recruit personnel for its own member agencies or for any other group abroad; nor does it make recommendations of individuals to any one of them. However, it does answer queries about overseas programs of voluntary groups, whether members or not. Write Technical Assistance Informal Clearing House, 200 Park Ave S., New York City, 10003.

The publication, *Overseas Programs of Private Non-Profit American Organizations* is not available to an individual. It was published in May, 1965 (Union Calendar, No. 178) as a report of the Subcommittee on International Organizations and Movements of the Committee on Foreign Affairs of the U.S. House of Representatives. It may be available in a large public library, or it is possible that your own Congressional representative may be able to get it for you. It is a nearly six-hundred-page presentation, in encyclopedic form, stating the objectives, type of personnel used, countries of operation, programs abroad, expenditures, source of funds, and exchange program, if any, for the period covered in the report.

Caution: Before your enthusiasm runs away with you, remember that not all organizations working abroad welcome applications beyond the threshold of the sixties. Some still count time by birthdays rather than individual strengths. Nor do all operate on a nonsectarian, nonracial basis. But there are a sufficient number that do disregard racial and religious lines, among them many who seize with alacrity the chance to get older people who have retained both health and skills, to warrant your making a serious effort to find exactly the one that will suit you and that will need you.

The Peace Corps

There is one organization working abroad officially under the umbrella of our State Department which gladly welcomes qualified men and women in the upper age brackets, and has done so ever since its inception in 1961. The official attitude of the Peace Corps remains the same as it was when expressed by its first Director, Sargent Shriver. He declared then, "We want as many capable older citizens as we can get." Two years after that there were nearly a hundred men and women enrolled who had already passed their fiftieth birthday, either in training or working for the Corps overseas. One seventy-year-old man was working in a tractor plant in Tunisia; a seventy-six-year-old engineer had gone to Pakistan. Two women, one sixty-five and the other sixty-four, were teaching in Ethiopia.

They were drawn to the Peace Corps through the same sense of service that motivated thousands of their younger colleagues. (There are still, on the average, over 60,000 applications from both young and old each year.)

Today much of the early flamboyance is gone, but older men and women are still joining with young ones to act as catalysts for self-help projects in underdeveloped areas of the world. When they leave, something of value is left behind that was not there when they arrived.

Creative ideas such as the Peace Corps are rare, and they draw both criticism and praise. On the whole, the 13,800 Corpsmen of both sexes overseas in 1968 (there were 30,000 in the first six years of the organization) represent America's potentially most effective instrument abroad to bring about social change and economic development. There have been failures, but they are far outweighed by the successes. In its still brief existence the Peace Corps has earned a reputation for diplomacy abroad, and has rendered vital assistance to fifty-nine countries in programs of health, education, and community development. As a result, requests for assistance have increased, and there is still a need for thousands, which the Corps hopes to add annually.

You may have heard that the work is rugged, the training period difficult, and isolation from friends and familiar surroundings hard to bear. Apparently none of this is too much for people like Mrs. Clara Rathjens and Oscar Haugan, the type of citizens who will be your co-aspirants if you apply and are accepted for training.

Mrs. Rathjens found her work as a teacher in Sierra Leone so satisfying she asked to have her stay extended. "Too much is made of hardships," she said. "If a person is in good health and can do his job in the United States he can do it in Africa, maybe even better." She proved it by staying five years.

Oscar Haugan was seventy-two when he completed two years as a heavy equipment operator in Tunisia. When he returned to the United States a member of the Peace Corps staff telephoned to discuss a television appearance. "It will have to be soon," said Mr. Haugan. "I'm going back into the Peace Corps. I leave for India next month."

Perhaps the best answer of all to any doubts that you may have about your own stamina or ability in a strange country was given by the Pickards. At seventy-eight Clarence Pickard (so far) is the oldest Peace Corps Volunteer. His wife, Mildred, aged seventy-three when they went to India, is not far behind him in anything, least of all vigor. They had been Iowa farmers. Asked why he and his wife "enlisted" for a two year term to show farmers in the Indian state of Uttar Pradesh how to raise more and better poultry and corn, this is what he said: "Just put yourself in our place. What would you have done? Our children had grown up; we had no financial handicap. So we rented our farm and toured different countries. We observed that lots of people our age had a time trying to get a kick out of life after they retired. We felt that we would get more enjoyment out of doing something useful than merely indulging ourselves trying to find entertainment. We had always worked in our lives and got more satisfaction out of what we achieved than we did just trying to have a good time."

More than five hundred people past fifty have served as Volunteers, and at least a dozen in their seventies, scattered among fifty-seven countries around the world, most of them where age is still considered a mark of wisdom. As Mrs. Emma Brodbeck, aged seventy-six observed when she went to the Philippines to teach, "A few gray hairs will take you a long way in the Orient."

If you would like to find out whether you, too, would be qualified, this is what you should take into account:

1. Any U.S. citizen above the age of eighteen is eligible; there is no upper age limit.

2. Good health is a necessary asset, but Peace Corps standards are flexible. The Peace Corps gives medical examinations to all potential volunteers and provides continuing medical service wherever they serve.

3. Married couples with no dependents under eighteen are encouraged to apply, but both must qualify as volunteers and they will be assigned to the same project.

4. It is not necessary to know a foreign language. A minimum of three hundred hours of language instruction is provided in a twelve- to fourteen-week training program (the Peace Corps staff teaches more than one hundred and fifty languages); frequently volunteers continue language study after they arrive on the job.

5. The Placement Test is an aid in evaluating your capabilities; no passing or failing grade is given.

6. Submission of an application in no way obligates you. Your final decision can be postponed till you are invited to enter training.

7. Training procedures have undergone much improvement since the early years. Some training is still carried on at college campuses in this country, more and more abroad, sometimes in the countries where the volunteers will serve. There are also training camps in Puerto Rico, the Virgin Islands, and Hawaii.

8. The physical training is rigorous but not impossible for older people. They are not expected to compete with younger ones. Most youngsters have a keen respect for the the tenacity and staying powers of their older companions. As one twenty-six-year-old said jokingly, "They have a separate program here for people over fifty, not because they can't keep up with us, but because we can't keep up with them!"

9. At most you can work for the Corps only five years. The normal tour of duty is from twenty to twenty-seven months, this can be extended one year. Or you can re-enroll for another two years, either in the same country or another. The Peace Corps is not a career.

10. Peace Corps officials have few doubts about the ability of older people to adapt themselves to living conditions. They vary. One elderly couple lived in a mud-brick house in an African village, but with time, work, patience, and some money from the Peace Corps they made it comfortable. A woman, a lively seventy-six-year-old, spent three teaching years in Ethiopia living in semi-luxury in a villa.

11. You will be paid an allowance to cover living expenses overseas, plus transportation costs, and coverage of medical care expense if that emergency arises. You are also paid $75 a month for the duration of your service but you will not receive it till you leave; it is considered a readjustment allowance. Its receipt does not affect any retirement or pension plan.

What do people think of their tour of duty when they come back? Most, old and young, regard it as a high point of experience.

"The call from countries all over the world for help in so many areas of work was the most challenging invitation we ever had," says Mrs. Henry Simmons. At the age of sixty-two, with her husband, then seventy-two, she spent two years in Tanzania, East Africa, teaching villagers and their children. "What most older pepole want is something that satisfies them, something for the heart, "says a sixty-five-year-old woman. When she retired from her Washington, D.C., job she carried on just such an affair of the heart for five years, first in Sierra Leone and then in Kenya, Africa.

Write for some of the literature. You do not need to commit yourself to more than an interest in receiving detailed information. For that or for an application blank, get in touch with

Senior Citizen Liaison
Specialized Recruiting
Peace Corps
Washington, D.C. 20525

American Business Volunteers

For a number of years American industry's involvement with the future well-being of small countries struggling for a place in the international sun has stimulated a kind of volunteer assistance that is a development characteristic only of our century. More and more practical aid to young industries in emerging nations carries with it the offer of volunteer service by experienced businessmen (and women) in a position to offer management and production skills without compensation, or merely for coverage of their expense disbursements.

This is giving a chance for a person who has achieved some success—not necessarily riches, but competence—in his own typically American field to put this experience at the disposal of those who cannot afford to pay for it in some foreign country. It is, in short, an opportunity for a retired businessman (or one who is beginning to cut down on his working time) to advise and consult, on a short-term basis. This kind of business missionary work leaves an enormous glow of satisfaction behind it and, in addition, is of genuine worth to our own country.

The International Executive Service Corps, the bulk of whose work is done by those no longer youthful, has been called by such colorful names as the "Businessman's Peace Corps," "the gray-flannel Peace Corps," and even the "gray-haired Peace Corps." What it is, however, is a sober effort to enlist support of the American business sector, so that talent can be provided to guide business firms in developing countries all around the world.

Since no program comparable to it had ever been attempted before, when the International Executive Service Corps was launched in 1964, backed by Federal support, there were many unanswered questions. Would the IESC be able to recruit volunteers willing to work beyond their retirement years, without pay? How long should an assignment last to be most beneficial to a client firm abroad? Would their own businessmen be interested enough to pay something for this kind of service?

After less than five years' operation the questions were all answered in the affirmative. The IESC does charge a modest monthly fee to the host country's applicants to cover living expenses and air fare for the man it sends, and his wife if he wants to take her. (Louise E. Barthold, a retired specialist in personnel practices, became the first woman volunteer, helping to evaluate an adult education curriculum in Brazil to promote cultural relations between that country and ours.) By 1968 over three hundred and thirty business firms in the United States were cooperating with IESC. They were helping, among other ways, by finding volunteers from their retired executives' ranks or lending persons still in their employ. Foreign firms were found to be willing to meet the small costs to insure topflight counseling. And finally, the IESC has found that the United States businessman (and often his wife to aid him) is patriotic and unselfish, ready to serve his country by showing how it achieves industrial success.

With the official blessing and financial support of the U.S. Agency for International Development and of leading corporations, a group in their fifties, sixties, and seventies have made accomplishments like these possible. They stayed, on the average, four months on an assignment:

A cannery in Iran improved its techniques and widened the variety of products it produced.

A distributor of drugs in Honduras learned how to revise his quality control and handling facilities.

A pulp and paper producer in Brazil reduced sharply the number of its rejected finished products.

Corps members aided a bakery in Thailand and reorganized a dress-manufacturing plant in Brazil. They have improved a dairy's operations in Iran and those of a bank in the Philippines.

In four years, more than twelve hundred companies in forty-two countries—from Chile to Ghana and from Lebanon to Korea—had found out how workers can be motivated, how new markets can be opened up, and how sales personnel have to be trained. Foreign firms take this type of advice gladly because those who give it are practical businessmen in their own field. One owner of a textile plant in Trinidad said, "We respect age here; the man who came to us carried with him the wisdom of years and experience."

Four hundred people completed overseas assignments in the first three years after the organization of the International Executive

Service Corps and then asked for a second one. As President Frank Pace, Jr. told a Senate Subcommittee on Aging, "They found fulfillment and rich satisfaction in this service at ages when many other retirees are languishing on the shelf."

Wives helped. Mrs. John G. Ormsby of Wilmington, North Carolina, a former accountant and bookkeeper, acted as her husband's secretary and helped set up accounting and office procedures for the new department store in Tripoli, Libya, that her husband was assigned to assist. Mrs. Roland W. Gleason of St. Petersburg, Florida, taught women in El Salvador knitting and paper-flower making, and with another IESC wife helped provide music in nursery school. Others have worked with orphaned and abandoned children, the blind, the handicapped, the retarded. They help leave behind them a good image of warmhearted, practical Americans.

The motives that impel retired businessmen to volunteer to advise, lead, and teach, but never to "boss" their counterparts abroad, are as various as the participants themselves. Omer C. Lunsford was the first man to be sent overseas by the IESC. An experienced oil company man who had "come up the hard way," he does not hide his idealism. He said of his twelve months in Central and South America, "I've always believed that being a good businessman is rendering a real service to your country; the IESC gives you a chance to broaden that service into new areas."

Siegfried Rosenthal of Cleveland went to Santa Catarina, Brazil, to share his knowledge with a food processor. He regards the counsel he gave there as part payment for the opportunities he found in the United States. When he was presented with a silver tray for his services he said, "I am especially touched because this is the anniversary of the day that I arrived in the United States fifty years ago, and today I am being recognized for service to my adopted country."

To be eligible all you need is a background of experience in such matters as production, cost control, marketing, personnel, financial administration, or technical experience on an administrative level. You can still be at work. If your firm has not already offered its cooperation to the International Executive Service Corps, it is possible it would be glad to cooperate with major corporations that have, and

171

in many instances are, releasing executives for leave-of-absence work. The IESC follows this procedure for recruitment:

1. When a request for assistance is received from a company abroad, the project must first be approved. Then a volunteer is sought; he must be someone whose background matches the job.

2. In the "skills bank" at IESC headquarters there are over 4,000 applications from people who want to volunteer for projects. The IESC wants to double that bank; there is room for you.

3. Volunteers serve without salaries. Sometimes the American business firm will pay a man on leave of absence. In any case, travel expenses are covered for a couple by IESC, plus a tax-exempt per diem rate for expenses abroad. This is no salary, but varies, since it is figured out according to the country of assignment, and is designed to cover all reasonable living expenses there.

4. Assignments occasionally end after a month or two but more often run to three or four months, sometimes somewhat longer. There can be a reassignment on request, but usually it is to another country.

5. Before leaving the USA a volunteer is thoroughly briefed on the nature of the company and its current problems, the country he is going to, and what he is supposed to accomplish. He can also avail himself of counsel from IESC specialists stationed in the general area. Support of business leaders in the country to which he is going is secured before he goes there.

6. Knowledge of the language of the country helps, but it is not obligatory. Reading books and reports in advance is advisable because it is bound to increase effectiveness and enjoyment based on understanding of local cultures.

A possible area of service was inaugurated in 1968 which offers another opportunity to qualified people on their return and may be of particular interest if you decide to apply. A supplementary "university program" has been developed by which some returned volunteers who have the requisite competence will be made available as on-campus speakers at various colleges and universities. The aim is twofold. It is expected that the program can aid in building a bridge between business and the academic world, and at the same time give students of college age a greater appreciation of what is going on in developing countries, and the opportunities available for those who may not be aware of them for possible business careers.

The place to apply is

Office of Executive Selection
International Executive Service Corps
545 Madison Avenue, New York, N.Y. 10022

You Do Not Have to Leave Home

Anybody who has the desire but neither the time nor a present possibility of offering his services abroad, and yet is vitally interested in aiding struggling nations through the application of American industrial methods, has a chance to do so through an organization sometimes described as a "mail-order Peace Corps."

Volunteers for International Technical Assistance (commonly known as VITA) came into existence at Schenectady, New York in the 1950's, largely as a result of the interest of local scientific personnel in aiding small nations solve their problems. The national headquarters continue to be on a college campus in the same city, and its small staff is aided by local volunteers who help with office chores and edit publications. Today requests for help come by mail from Africa, Asia, and Latin America, and are answered by correspondence with qualified volunteers all over the country. They either work individually or in teams and then mail their solutions to the inquirer, so that VITA complements work done by other American organizations and there is no conflict of interests.

Any scientist, technician, engineer, educator, businessman (or woman), farmer—or any other qualified person—is invited to offer his or her services to answer queries that arise and have to be made by people trying to raise living standards in underdeveloped parts of the world. Queries come in, not only from natives of the country, but from United Nations field workers, Peace Corps volunteers, government functionaries from the United States, missionaries, teachers, agriculturists—or anybody else working to better local conditions, including American businessmen overseas.

The questions asked by mail are sorted at the Schenectady headquarters and then forwarded to the person or group that can best answer them. This is not as difficult as it seems because detailed resumés of skills listed by volunteers are kept on file in a central "bank" in Schenectady.

VITA has a place for you if you can do one of two things or both: (1) Give information in simple, concise, easily understood terms on some technical matter. Since queries cover a very wide range, this allows much latitude. (2) Have the ability to work out designs for basic devices that can be built at small cost with locally available materials in a foreign country.

To give you an idea of the problems presented, here is a sampling (taken from the VITA *Newsletter,* sent to all participants in the work). Note they are listed in want-ad fashion.

Frog farming. Information needed on how to raise meat-producing frogs that can thrive in the tropical climate of El Salvador, and a list of growers who can supply males and females, tad poles, or even eggs.

Selection of breeds. A Peace Corpsman in the Amazon valley wanted advice on selection of breeds of chickens, ducks, rabbits, hogs, turkey, and cattle.

Educational materials. A missionary from Burundi asked about educational materials for nurse's training and information on parasite control.

Managerial advice. The manager of a cement brick-making cooperative in Panama sought technical information and managerial advice.

Breadfruit storage. A county extension agent in Jamaica says people need a way to store breadfruit, which is now eaten only in season.

Design for bookcart. Also in Jamaica, a Peace Corps volunteer wants plans for "a light, durable, maneuverable—and above all else, quiet—bookcart to serve a 65-bed hospital."

174

There is often a friendly correspondence that results from queries like these which opens windows of enlightenment on both sides. For instance an Indian citizen who was a radio officer operating out of Singapore wanted advice on how to manufacture resistors. His request included a plea for a bibliography of reference books and technical journals that would help him help himself. He received both the books and the lists; who can say which person was the chief gainer?

The volunteer who extends himself to give a slight personal touch to his directions becomes meaningful to the inquirer, who may be, like the Reverend Jerry Smyth, both isolated and frustrated when he sees a problem but not its solution. The lively pile of letters that passed between Mr. Smyth and various VITA volunteers who helped him with plans to develop an agricultural school in Brazil is over four inches deep. As he said, the school's only endowment was some two thousand undeveloped acres.

Volunteers may be in business, a university, an organization, or may have retired from any one of them. Where there are enough people with knowledge along diverse lines, they form themselves into a chapter. If you join one, you will find yourself in stimulating company. For instance a small tractor, made chiefly from used automobile parts, was the development of the New Holland, Pennsylvania, chapter. This is a typical "make-do" device, intended for people who can learn how to produce it for themselves with limited local resources.

There is also another stimulating possibility of making a contribution important enough to have permanent value. Some information collected or devised by volunteers already is being published. Their aim is to meet rural development needs in countries where "going to the store to get a part" is a next to impossible dream. Two *Village Technology Handbooks* have already been published. Their content consists of the practical information offered by VITA's volunteers. They contain such basic information as "how to dig and case a well," and "how to build a handpowered grain mill." The U. S. Agency for International Development had them published and translated into Spanish and French, but it was VITA's volunteers who translated them into Hindi. The books are already part of the basic material in the book lockers sent by the Peace Corps to its regional offices.

You do not have to have esoteric knowledge to become a VITA volunteer. Send your request for information or a resumé (and ask for the address of the nearest chapter) to

Volunteers for International Technical Assistance, Inc.
College Campus, Schenectady, N.Y. 12308

Volunteering Under Religious Auspices

Everybody is familiar with the long and honorable history of missionaries in foreign lands, but the layman whose work parallels but does not duplicate the professional church-supported missionary is a comparatively new development, born out of the increasing difficulty of maintaining traditional structures in a world in which past separations of geography and distance are rapidly fading out, a volunteer may not be a member of the church or denomination that sends him, or for that matter, not even a Christian.

Today's volunteer is working under such auspices as World Neighbors or Crossroads Africa, or the local church back home. He may be feeding refugees in Biafra, setting up an adoption agency for war orphans in Jordan, sitting at a desk in an African town discussing with local tribal leaders the best way to build a road or a bridge, directing the clearance of a swamp-infested area somewhere in Asia—in short, he may be everywhere. For, as one great churchman has said, "The needs around today's world call not only for engineers who will build bridges of steel but also bridges of understanding."

Not every organization, however, is willing to accept the fact that today's elders are apt to have as much stamina, energy, and endurance (coupled with wisdom) as the young man or woman fired with a dream of reclaiming the world's waste areas. But the number is growing who recognize that the retired person, or the about to be retired man or woman, is a potential source of great strength; they disregard age and concentrate only on possibilities of achieving an end. Invariably, these are the organizations that are nonsectarian and interracial in a sincere desire to find the right person.

176

WORKING UNDER AUSPICES OF LAOS

LAOS—as a newspaper man once quipped, "a commitment, not a country"—came into being largely as the result of one man's idealism and much hard work. It grew out of the experiences Robert B. Kochtitzky had as a volunteer abroad while he was still a theological seminary student. As soon as he graduated he set about forming LAOS (the letters form the Greek word that the New Testament uses in reference to all the people of God) . That was in 1962. In the next three years over a hundred and fifty volunteers—all recruited on a nondenominational basis—had contributed over thirty years of combined service on four continents. One of them was a retired surgeon from Miami, Florida. That he was also a Jew had nothing to do with the fact that he filled a vacant post in a mission hospital overseas; he was accepted for his abilities, not his religious beliefs.

LAOS is governed by an interdenominational board. It functions on the theory that if you properly challenge laymen and offer them the right kind of post for an outlet for their talents you get a response from many who have a month, a summer, a year—or any other period —they are willing to give some place overseas (or in this country, too) , regardless of what church auspices they will be working under.

LAOS operates on a frugal budget raised from contributions by individuals, national denominational boards, and churches. Much of its office work in the modest headquarters in Jackson, Mississippi, is also contributed. The dedication of its staff and board is one reason that teachers, nurses, dentists, physicians, engineers, agriculturists, and a host of other men and women ask to have their applications reviewed. Here are some factual reasons for their interest and why it may be worth your own investigation:

1. LAOS calls itself a service agency "consciously Christian, but ecumenical, non-denominational." For the Jew and Gentile, Protestant and Catholic, there is equal welcome.

2. LAOS has no projects of its own; all qualifications for a vacancy are set by the agency making the request, and all subsequent agreements are between it and the volunteer, once he or she is accepted.

3. A personal interview is desirable but not obligatory. Applications must be accompanied by six letters of reference and a medical

statement. Once approved, the applicant is matched to the appropriate vacancy.

4. Most openings can provide the volunteer with no more than housing; a few offer board as well as room; some will give help in footing transportation expenses; an even smaller number can give a small stipend for long-term service.

5. Much of the growth in numbers of volunteers is due to the person-to person publicity growing out of twenty-five talks each returned volunteer is asked to give. It is also hoped he will raise $100 for continued recruitment purposes.

6. Pre-orientation consists of a reading list provided by LAOS; sometimes it is possible to participate in a short orientation course like one at the Ecumenical Institute in Chicago.

LAOS fills posts in Africa, Asia, and South America (as well on occasion in the United States) for service periods ranging from a month to a year or more. Here are samplings of openings listed in one issue of LAOS's bimonthly, characteristically named *Leaven*. The "want ads" in this issue were confined to South America, but in subsequent ones similar posts were listed for Asia and Africa. If your choice should be for one or the other, state it, and wait your turn.

Puerto Rico: Vacancies for teachers, medical doctors, dentists, nurses, farm workers, social workers, youth workers

Chile: Posts open for persons with carpentry and plumbing experience, taxidermist, English teacher, Spanish-speaking librarian, commercial teacher, dentist, physician

Mexico: Wanted: carpenter, playground director, secretary, social worker, dentist; cooperative housing administrator, nurses, pharmacist, x-ray technician

And so on, through the gamut of life's necessities. If you, too, have good health, and a willingness to continue to use your occupational skill (including such tasks as housemother or cook) and you are looking for meaningful service abroad, write LAOS. Though the agency that has an opening will probably be related to a Christian denomination, no special religious qualifications or duties will be asked of you. The address is

> Laymen's Overseas Service, Inc.
> Post Office Box 5031
> Jackson, Mississippi 39216

USING MEDICAL AND ALLIED SKILLS

On occasion, volunteers who do not fit into what LAOS requires at the particular time they have to give have been referred to other overseas agencies, including the Catholic Medical Mission Board. In spite of its name, the men and women it sends overseas as volunteers do *not* have to be Catholics, and very often are not. They do serve in Catholic-sponsored hospitals and clinics in Africa, Asia, Central and South America. The only "ministry" required of them there is that their skills be used on behalf of the sick poor. The Board acts as a clearinghouse in the following ways:

1. Placements are confined to medical personnel of all kinds—dentists, physicians, pharmacists, medical technologists, and so on.

2. Applications are accepted from anybody who has the requisite skills. He will be screened through references, a physical examination, and a psychological evaluation.

3. CMMB tries to match the preferences, as well as the qualifications of the volunteer with the needs of Catholic hospitals, clinics, and dispensaries abroad.

4. Preference is given to institutions in which the volunteer can participate in the training of natives in medical skills so that something lasting can be left behind.

5. Age is *not* a factor; what you have to have is some kind of medical background, plus what the Board defines as a "congenial, well-integrated personality, endless patience and compassion."

6. The Board believes one of its major functions must be to supply medicines and medical equipment to institutions in developing countries. Nevertheless, since equipment in many places is still meager, old-fashioned, or simply nonexistent, the ability to improvise and at the same time to try to maintain acceptable standards is an essential quality.

7. If you have only a vacation month or two to give, or want to try out a short-term before you enroll for a long one, the Board will omit the physical examination and the psychological evaluation, if you are otherwise qualified.

8. Expenses are sometimes met by a hospital that urgently needs medical experts; usually nothing more than housing is provided; occasionally board and room is covered. Some "scholarships" are available through local churches and foundations in this country. It is more usual to have to invest your own money for transportation and part of your living expenses after you arrive.

Who are the people who find this kind of work rewarding? The fact that they do is found in the enrollment and re-enrollment of so many man-and-wife teams. The Rosenbergs of New York City are one; they donated their medical services to Maryknoll Hospital in Guatemala one year, and to a hospital in the Windward Islands the next. "Give us a hospital with an acute need for our skills and a heavy patient overload to assure maximum use of our respective talents," Dr. Conrad Rosenberg wrote on his first application. And when they came back from their second, "The best vacation we ever had!" he said.

Out in Okinawa, Dr. Michael Kolcum is enrolled for a three-year period at a dispensary, and has taken on additional duties in Boy Scout work. He was a sixty-eight-year-old Virginia dentist whose wife is as happy as he is; she teaches in an elementary school. Single individuals enroll and re-enroll by the hundreds. Veronica Rowan, X-ray technician, became a short-term worker in Guatemala immediately after she retired from the Newark, New Jersey, school system. At seventy-one she took on a two months' tour of duty at a hospital in St. Lucia and voluntarily extended it "because the need was so great."

180

Reflecting the conviction of the Catholic Medical Mission Board that the healing of mankind should be on a completely nonracial, nonsectarian basis, fellow members of the First Unitarian Church of Providence, Rhode Island, contributed $500 for Dr. H. Frederick Stephens to spend for instruments and pharmaceutical and operating supplies. He and Mrs. Stephens spent their first tour of duty at St. Jude's Hospital in St. Lucia. Dr. Stephens, an ophthalmologist, held morning clinics and operated during afternoons. Mrs. Stephens vision-screened school children, trained student nurses to do the same, and gave talks on eye health and safety. Patients increased via the "bamboo telephone" from ten the first day to seventy-two a week later. When he came back Dr. Stephens wrote:

> We were there to help and were very busy. It was interesting work and we encourage other physicians, dentists, nurses, technicians, and pharmacists (and their mates) to come—all with a talent, a motivation, a willingness to serve, a spirit of adaptability, good health and a sense of fun. . . . It's great! You will enjoy the work!

Dr. Stephens followed his own advice and repeated with his wife their term of duty the following year, again taking supplies. He also persuaded the hospital in which he is the Chief of the Department of Ophthalmology to allow his senior resident, Dr. Reid Appleby, to finish his own residency at St. Jude's Hospital and take his wife along as a medical secretary. Dr. Stephen's son, also an ophthalmologist, caught the family enthusiasm, and then spent five weeks at St. Jude with his wife, a nurse, to help him. (Incidentally, none of the group is Catholic.)

Short-term volunteers can be placed without much preliminary paper work. The time required to match long-term volunteers to the waiting post takes from three to six months. For information and an application blank, query

Placement Director
Catholic Medical Mission Board, Inc.
10 West 17th Street, New York, N.Y. 10011

Working for MEDICO

If you feel you would rather offer your services to a lay organization, and are medically qualified, apply to MEDICO. It was founded by the late Dr. Thomas Dooley and became a part of CARE, the nonsectarian medical service that provides aid to newly developing countries. Before he volunteered through the Catholic Medical Mission Board, Dr. Stephens had served a month as a volunteer under MEDICO, at the Beni Mesous Hospital in Algeria. As usual, his wife went with him. Although she describes herself as "not para-medically trained," she says, "Women can always find plenty to do to help; all you need is initiative, willingness, and cooperation." Mrs. Stephens proved it by typing and taking care of medical records and running errands, and she even learned to be a scrub nurse in the operating room while she was in Algeria.

MEDICO has no age limit for short-term volunteers like the Stephens couple. The organization welcomes trained specialists and retired medical personnel—or semi-retirees. No salary is paid, and volunteers pay their own living expenses and transportation. A month is the ordinary period of service. Many practitioners, and often their wives, have found satisfaction in giving a month to serving in areas that, medically speaking, may be barren, and so in great need.

Address queries to

MEDICO, 600 First Avenue
New York, N.Y. 10016

Working Under Church Auspices

If you would like to work overseas for the denomination that means most to you, there is no dearth of opportunity. The needs are great and the way to service is open to those who have skills to give and who have, or can secure, the money to cover expenses. For instance, the Commission on Ecumenical Mission and Relations, United Presbyterian Church in the U.S.A., defines a volunteer as "someone who offers his (or her) skills and abilities to fill a requested need for assistance, and who is responsible for the financial obligations involved."

The type of roles generally fall into these categories. *Note:* The examples cited were actual calls for help.

1. *Assistance given during vacation or furlough of regular missionary personnel.* Examples: (a) accountant needed for a hospital in Yucatan for two months; (b) business manager needed in Korean hospital during furlough of Superintendent, especially in relation to cost accounting procedures, stock control, and so forth.

2. *Professional assistance for periods of short duration.* Examples: (a) architect needed, two months or longer, for Medical Center in India (b) dentist; one month or more, hospital in Brazil.

3. *Temporary assistance while longer-term personnel (the latter salaried) is sought.* The gamut ran from "an experienced Christian Education worker for leadership training" needed in Korea to a request from a mission that wants a "Spanish-speaking dentist (or one prepared to hire an interpreter) to teach as well as practice" in Guatemala.

4. *Assistance beyond the capacity of current budgets and staffs in institutions.* The greatest needs still seem to be physicians, doctors, and nurses, as well as teachers. But mechanics, carpenters, electrical and metal workers, pressmen, social workers are needed somewhere. The most favored age is twenty-one to forty, but there are exceptions for anyone free of chronic ailments; the maximum age limit varies with the individual case.

There is nothing unusual about a lay man or woman going for a short or long time without monetary recompense to help people living in poverty, disease, or ignorance in faraway countries. It is a tradition as old as the church itself. Today, however, in spite of more than extensive plenty in some areas of the world, needs in others are greater. Furthermore, mounting populations and diminishing numbers of clergy mean that the latter, weighed down with chores and labors outside their concern for the spirit, vitally need and appreciate an offer of lay help.

If, as one semi-retired surgeon put it, you want "to collaborate with other Christians, Jews, Hindus, Moslems, Buddhists, and nonbelievers in the common service of humanity" (he did, in India, and sums it up by saying "I had a tremendously rewarding experience which I'm sure I shall never forget"), talk it over with a pastor or priest. You do not have to be a member of the congregation. To help you make up your mind, send for the leaflet *What Is Volunteer Service?* It gives in fifteen succinct, practical answers, information anyone will find useful. It answers questions like these:

Where may I serve? Do I have a choice?
Does being a volunteer mean I must pay all the expenses involved?
How long after I apply may I expect to know the result?
What about medical clearance?
Are my expenses as a volunteer tax deductible? and so on.

For information, write

Service Desk for Volunteers, Room 921
Commission on Ecumenical Mission and Relations
United Presbyterian Church in the U.S.A.
475 Riverside Drive, New York, N.Y. 10027
(You need not be a member of that denomination.)

The spirit of ecumenical approaches to giving is growing stronger each day. So you can also learn from this suggestive series of questions posed by the Catholic Medical Mission Board for anybody who wants to concern himself with people in need in a country strange to him:

How have I lived my life up to now?
Am I annoyed by change, or do I adapt easily to situations?
Do I see people and things the way they are, and try to understand them in their differences?
Or do I see them the way I would like them to be?
Am I capable of improvising, inventing, changing my program?
Do I have good judgment, without haste or panic?
Am I capable of an overall evaluation of things, relying on reason rather than on impulsive personal reactions?
Do I need others? Do I like to converse?

Am I capable of listening and of trying to understand?

Do I know how to enter into dialogue, ready to receive as much as to give?

Preparing for Life Overseas

Success in work abroad often depends on the extent of one's pre-travel preparation. This is true whether you work for international, governmental, private, or religious organizations. The essential for all of them, regardless of age, is teamwork and collaboration both with your own nationals and with the people you have come to help. While you may receive more respect in the far corners of the world because of your gray hairs than your juniors do, you will still have to have a knowledge of the host country's political, social, religious, and economic heritage if you want to be effective. It goes without saying you also must have respect for its culture and sensitivity toward the ways its people express it.

Every organization will help you prepare yourself. Some make literature available and arrange study conferences; many enlist the cooperation of governmental officials who will know intimately the region to which you are going and what conditions you will live and work under. A few will help you attain a working knowledge of the language you will hear. Even if you are offering only a month or two of your time, the more prepared you are to receive—as well as to give—the greater will be your chance not only of doing what you came to perform, but of achieving rich personal growth and storing up memories that will outlast your sojourn.

Chapter IX

Creating Your Own Opportunities

Nobody who has reached the age of fifty has to be convinced by scientists or medical authorities that his hopes of being happy in his sixties, seventies, or eighties very largely depend on how active—above all, how mentally active—he is. The wise ones know that if they begin or continue to do some things that promote the well-being of their fellowman the chances are they are also going to find personal gratification. But it would be an exaggeration to say that every community and every organization holds out an eager hand to the would-be volunteer past middle age. Programs that require a long-term change in public attitudes take time, and this is no less true for outmoded prejudices toward the abilities of the aging than it is for the problems of racism and poverty.

Nevertheless, all through the United States men and women, determined that they will not let their talents ossify as they get older, are doing something about it. If the way they have chosen is not clear, or the manner in which they would like to give their services clogged, many of them have banded together to create a new community organization.

It will not be difficult for you to find out about people who have taken the bit into their own mouths at a period well along in life, because their ventures are well publicized not only locally, but in national magazines.

The philosophy behind many of these valiant attempts at new solutions to their own as well as community problems, was once summed up in an unorthodox fashion by a man neither well educated nor past executive of anything. He is a member of Boston's nonprofit Civic Center and Clearing House, founded by a man who refused to be bound by conventions.

"You Can Have a Tomorrow," was the title of the article. It outlined the purpose of the organization in these words:

> We wish to do what we can to produce a society in which non-work, that is work or effort without money wages, will hold at least as much challenge, respectability, possibility for growth and self-enrichment, opportunity for pride in accomplishment, opportunity for advancement in responsibility, as paid work.

If you are one of those who have searched for ways of satisfaction that do not necessarily lead to money returns, and have not found exactly the ones you want to pursue, it is quite likely others feel the same way, particularly if they are in the near-retirement or post-retirement age group. You do not have to live in a large metropolis or even have a wide circle of business or professional acquaintances or friends to broach an idea that may attract them, if there is a valid reason for a new organization's existence in your town. Ideas born in a flash of insight or inspiration by one person with imagination can drew answering sparks from others provided the ideas possess the germ of both usefulness and practicality.

You can familiarize yourself with at least some of the projects that have been launched, with neither tremendous effort nor on a grand scale, by members of your own age group. All you have to do is write a few letters and enclose some postage stamps. You will find a willingness to share experiences on the part of retired people who have developed their own routes to fields of service. If they have received many previous queries (which happens when a venture receives national publicity) you may even be supplied with printed literature or a mimeographed blueprint for action. But whether by letter or by formal outline, you will find information that will help you avoid whatever pitfalls may lurk through over-optimism and under-preparation.

If nothing else, interchange of correspondence will give you heartening evidence that people all over the United States are demonstrating that aging is a time of life that does not automatically cancel out initiative.

You will find that many of these organizations came into being because there is a gulf that some in their later years often have great difficulty crossing. Many community efforts made by retired people, therefore, are compassionate attempts to help those of their own generation cross that gulf to obtain work, better housing, overcome the ills of being homebound or loneliness—or some other obstacle the forlorn old often face.

Sources of General Information

As a preliminary to your own search, therefore, find out what, if anything has been started by older men and women with new ideas in your own state. The best source of information is the state commission, council, or committee on aging. (See Appendix.)

The major source nationally is the Federal Administration on Aging. Its closest source to you will be a Regional Office to which you are entitled to apply for counsel and information. (See Appendix for addresses.)

The official publication, *Aging,* a monthly, often carries stories of active older people who are participating in the life of their community, in addition to information of interest to anybody who wants to be abreast of everything happening in the way of new legislation, new experiments, and new developments that affect older Americans. You will find *Aging* in practically any good public library, or you can subscribe:

> *Aging*
> Superintendent of Documents
> U.S. Printing Office
> Washington, D.C. 20402 ($2.00)
> Sample copies, 20 cents each

Equally important, if you are interested in outstanding projects conducted by (or in behalf of) older men and women, is the Administration's continuing series entitled *Design for Action for Older Americans*. This consists of four-page, loose-leaf descriptions written in nontechnical style for the layman. Note this significant description of their purpose: "The project reports contain sufficient details to enable you to determine whether a similar project, adapted to the situation in your community, should be undertaken. Names of individuals from whom additional information may be obtained are included."

This last feature alone would make them worthwhile looking at. Single copies are free; write for a list of all current titles. Address Administration on Aging, Washington, D.C. 20201.

Once you have this general background, then begin to supplement it by correspondence with some leaders in other communities who have successfully introduced new ideas into their hometowns. You will find it is their initiative, not their financial status, or backing, which has been the deciding factor. Not all these projects have to do with bringing more ease into the life of other older men and women, but a sufficient number of them do to make it a matter of common sense for you to find out why. Even if you decide you would prefer to turn your efforts in another direction, the methods used to arouse attention and secure community interest merit your attention.

Help to the Over-Sixty Group

Much of the compassion shown their fellow citizens by older people who do not need aid themselves is going out to the man or woman still struggling to make financial needs match inadequate incomes from pensions, savings, or welfare department allowances. Because the situation becomes more acute as one grows older, many new civic enterprises are the ingenious efforts of more fortunate men and women in upper age brackets to uncover jobs and get unprejudiced hearings for the unemployed old whose chief desire is to preserve their independence as long as they are able.

If you wonder why there is any necessity to have special counseling and employment-hunting agencies for elderly applicants the reasons

189

are not hard to find, although Federal and state employment offices are free to any applicant and readily available. In addition many, particularly in large cities, have specially trained employees who make a special effort to overcome the resistance that exists in many places and in many companies to hiring not only men or women in their sixties but those still in their forties or fifties. Yet mark this: The U. S. Department of Labor realistically notes in its reports that "employers' preferred hiring age is generally twenty-one to forty-five." (They do not call it the "ideal" hiring age, but you can draw your own conclusions.)

Careful, regular unemployment records kept by the Department of Labor indicate "a large proportion" (in some reports the figure 45 percent is used) of workers past forty-five who lose their jobs remain unemployed for fifteen to thirty-five weeks. Men and women past fifty encounter particularly great resistance, regardless of their physical fitness, mental ability, or years of experience. (The articulate have sometimes written of their surprise and shock, and you will find their books in a public library.)

This is a nationwide, not a local situation, and it is prevalent not only during hard times but during a high period of national prosperity. The "it can't happen here" philosophy is therefore ostrich-like. Those concerned individuals—many of them prosperous older people—who are aware of what has happened locally, in spite of many legal attempts to overcome the situation, have themselves resolved to help older applicants overcome bugaboos local employers fear. Because they have the time and the deep concern to deal individually with the applicant's qualifications and educate individual employers, some of the new small civic enterprises are successful in overcoming objections raised on unproved grounds by local business enterprises.

If you are aware of the long-awaited Age Discrimination Employment Act, which went into effect in the summer of 1968, you may wonder why such special agencies are needed. For the first time the law does make it impossible for employers, labor unions, or employment agencies to place "help wanted" advertisements specifying age as a qualification for a job. There are legal penalties intended to enforce the law, so that no person may be discharged or barred from work simply because he has reached a certain calendar age.

Undeniably this is an important step forward in recognition of the fact that aging men and women are still people who differ from one another. Theoretically the law is intended to extend opportunities for a person between forty and sixty-five to continue to use his abilities and experience for pay. Nevertheless, no one believes the law will bring about Utopia. One reason is that it affects only employers of twenty-five or more persons in an industry affecting interstate commerce. The more subtle reason is that employers can still exercise prejudices against prospective employes on disproved grounds and stay within the law. For instance, the accusations most frequently cited as barriers by personnel heads who look askance at an application for unseen men and women past fifty, are likelihood of ill health, possibility of frequent absenteeism, tendency to accidents, low production rate as compared with the young, and—most damning of all because it is the most difficult to combat without a chance to disprove it—the inability to change habits of work or be versatile.

It follows that a man's or woman's skills still have to be "sold" in many instances by someone who cares enough to demonstrate a particular individual does not fall into a slot of "unsuitability" and deserves a trial. That is where the voice of an experienced older person, himself or herself not in need of an employer's consideration, counts most. So many who are not interested in adding to their own incomes have begun to work in their own communities for people of their own generation who do need to be employed for pay.

A cogent reason can be found in the statement made by Senator Harrison A. Williams, Chairman of the Senate Special Committee on Aging. In 1967 he declared that there were more than 19,000,000 citizens in the United States over 60 years of age, and that 50 percent of them were poor. It is not likely the situation has changed radically.

The new ventures into compassion carried on by people of your own generation should make you realize that sensitivity and human interest will exist even in what sometimes seems to be a "devil-take-the-hindmost" world. They are organized and sometimes subsidized by people determined that they will not waste their own most precious resources, the wisdom that comes only with experience, and the experience that can come only with time. The ideas they have originated to meet local problems are diverse. But each emphasizes that the turn of the page on the calendar which marks a sixty-fifth birthday does not really signalize a dimunition of one's ability (or inability) to do something, and that something can be more than what used to be called "boondoggling."

NORWALK'S SENIOR PERSONNEL PLACEMENT BUREAU

The chief reason to start your investigation with a Bureau that began in January, 1966, in Norwalk, Connecticut, is not because nearly one out of ten in its population of approximately 85,000 is past 65 years old. It is because, in this sprawling town that covers 22 square miles, a Senior Personnel Placement Bureau was started which the Administration on Aging believes can serve as a pattern for similar efforts elsewhere. To find out in detail about it, send for

"A Project Study on Employment Referral"
Designs for Action for Older Americans
Publication 904, April, 1967 (free)
Administration on Aging, Washington, D.C. 20201

It was Lawrence Hochheimer, a retired manufacturer, who dedicated himself to the idea of doing something about finding employment for older people who needed it, at least in his own community and its environs. He gathered around him hardheaded businessmen, like himself. They included a banker, and an advertising executive, and some others, all retired and all with experience in civic work.

They had no money, and it was Mr. Hochheimer who donated the sum necessary to provide for initial operating expenses, including stationery, stamps, and printing of a widely distributed placard to acquaint both employers and would-be employers with the nonprofit organization, which had a charter from the state of Connecticut.

The Senior Personnel Placement Bureau's first success was in securing the cooperation of the Chamber of Commerce. The latter provided office space, supplies, a telephone, and some staff assistance that was helpful before the Bureau enrolled its own volunteer staff (all retirees). It was the Chamber that was also persuaded by the seventy-one-year-old Mr. Hochheimer and his associates to circulate news

192

about the qualifications of the first sixteen job-seekers to employers with a covering letter emphasizing the mutual advantages in getting a qualified worker and providing a job for a reliable older person. (The letter advised that all clients had been interviewed and screened; they included nine men with experience ranging from accountant to butcher, and seven women with backgrounds in everything from baby-sitting to fashion consultation.) The Chamber helped the infant organization get over another hurdle; it emphasized in its covering letter that older applicants were willing to waive inclusion in any company's benefit plan.

From the outset, the fact that volunteers, themselves older men and women, conducted the interviews with applicants inspired confidence. Records have been kept punctiliously; clients are requested, when they come, to indicate whether they want full-time, part-time, day, or night work, and openings are sought accordingly by volunteers (not always the same who man the office). They make a special effort to interview personnel managers, or others who are empowered to do hiring, in order to impress on those who have never hired the above-forty-five groups that they may be missing something. In the course of their telephoning and their personal visits they uncover possible openings; after six months the Bureau reported it had secured employment for sixty men and women. This was sufficient to permit the Board to apply to the Connecticut State Commission on Services for Elderly Persons for a grant. When it was secured through the Older Americans Act, the Senior Personnel Placement Bureau was able to move out of its crowded quarters into its own modest office. Its next needed step was to hire a paid clerk-typist to care for mounting work. The one who took over the job (a retiree, of course) agreed to work four hours a day, five days a week.

For anyone who has to start his own venture with small funds and untried and unpaid help, it is worthwhile remarking that when the Commission was considering a grant it estimated the personal service of volunteers in the office and on their job-hunts as covering 60 percent of the cost of operation. The Bureau goes on expanding into new channels, every one of which is designed to make the lives of Connecticut's elderly men and women in the vicinity of Norwalk richer (and not necessarily only in money).

TUCSON'S ON-CALL EMPLOYMENT RESERVE

At the other end of the country, in Tucson, Arizona, TOCER, which is short for "Tucson On-Call Employment Reserve," illustrates that it is possible to function on a budget considerably under a yearly five thousand dollars and to begin with next to nothing.

TOCER antedates most similar organizations so that it has already proved, as one of its volunteers said, "all you need is an empty storeroom, a few pieces of furniture, and some dedicated persons. Then you can start an 'On-Call Employment Reserve' in your own town."

That volunteer was Mrs. Beatrice C. Douglas, an ex-newspaperwoman from New Jersey, who walked into TOCER hoping to find work; and while she did do some free-lancing after that, her main job became dedicated hours given over to helping man the office at TOCER.

Tucon's On-Call Employment Reserve started in 1956 with the sole purpose of helping middle-aged, elderly, and handicapped men and women find jobs. It has never deviated from that purpose in spite of the fact that it has functioned chiefly on goodwill and devotion. (In 1968 its budget was $4,000) When Mrs. Douglas came to it a few years ago, TOCER was still occupying a single room in an old building. The furniture was secondhand and sparse. Everything, including the office space, had been donated. But if the physical surroundings are still unpretentious, the results are not.

Over the years volunteers have regularly given hours every week to counseling, telephoning, interviewing applicants and employers, and making placements. In 1967 22 of them piled up 4,090 hours of work without pay. They found 379 jobs and made 1,217 referrals of applicants to offices, stores and shops, schools, homes, farms, and ranches, all in the Tucson area. In addition, 8,200 individuals secured some kind of service by telephone; another 1,640 came directly to the office to find out what they wanted to know.

Much of the success is due to the enterprise of the volunteer Executive Director, Charles H. McCausland, who retired from the insurance field after thirty-two years of business experience in it, and put all his energies to work at TOCER. Today he says, "It's my only business!" He started as a Field Representative when the office opened in 1956, and became its volunteer Executive Director in 1960.

TOCER began as an effort launched by public-spirited citizens in Tucson primarily to help those who came in search of health or in their retirement years, and subsequently found their incomes inadequate. Most of them are people who want only part-time jobs; the majority find a clearinghouse like TOCER easier to approach than a regular employment agency, partly because those behind the desks are people like themselves. (There is only one paid employee—a part-time clerk-typist, herself handicapped.)

TOCER has gone back to its original method of financing; those who have watched it over the years are of the opinion it will continue to find enough individual donors to insure its usefulness for some time to come. It is heartening proof that you do not have to have a Federal grant, or even be included in a community fund, if you have an idea and a purpose, and are a member of a really devoted group who wants to work to realize its goals.

OVER-60 EMPLOYMENT AND COUNSELING SERVICE

There are several features about the Over-60 Employment and Counseling Service of Northern Virginia (located in Arlington) which make it worth looking at from the point of view of your own community.

In the first place, it was actually created in January, 1956, because the year before members of a "Silver Age Club," all sixty or over, said they wanted and needed an employment service that would be specially geared to helping older people find jobs.

Arlington County, near Washington, D.C., is the home of many retired government workers. Other older people move there to be near their adult children. Still others grew up and stayed there. The Silver Age Clubs are sponsored by the Department of Recreation and Parks, and they made their desire for a special employment service known to the Department. The reasons they gave are applicable to practically any community:

To supplement their reduced income and cope with inflationary costs

To render a service to the community

To continue growing in wisdom and usefulness

To achieve a feeling of belongingness

To maintain high morale

To be able to continue a life of independence, personal dignity, and self-respect

With the cooperation of various community organizations, the Soroptimist and Venture clubs, and the Department of Recreation and Parks, the Over-60 Employment and Counseling Service of Arlington County was formally inaugurated to carry out the aims so articulately expressed by Silver Age Club members.

One feature incorporated into the program of Arlington County's Over-60 Employment Counseling Service could be adopted anywhere. In recognition of the desire of every human being to feel he can be of worth to his fellows at any age, during counseling interviews suggestions are made regarding volunteering. If the applicant is interested he or she is handed a list that has this heading:

Volunteers Needed

Do you sometimes wonder if there are things you could do for others in the community, but feel at a loss to learn where your services would be most effective? Here is a list of places where your time and talents are needed.

The organizations listed are carefully screened to be certain that people over sixty will be welcomed as volunteers. The range is wide enough to include usual opportunities (the type that exist everywhere—e.g., reading to the blind, taking residents of retirement homes shopping, visiting the shut-in). In addition, there are more unusual opportunities, such as an invitation to help with receptions given for foreign visitors at the Washington International Center.

OVER-60 EMPLOYMENT COUNSELING SERVICE OF MARYLAND

Not all older people are as articulate as the ones in Arlington who first formulated their "demands," but the same needs exist in much larger places; they are more acute in large cities where the woes of the unemployed old are severe.

Baltimore's Over-60 Employment Counseling Service was set up to combat such difficulties. It originated in 1962 through the efforts of just one civic-minded individual who brought together a group from various walks of life to form the original Board of Governors. When operation commenced in April, 1963, the new agency was housed in what was formerly the boiler room of the parish house of St. Paul's Episcopal Church. But after four and a half years' operation 3,650 people had been counseled (some many times), about 2,000 placements had been made, and approximately 24,000 hours of volunteer service given. The people restored to usefulness and productivity ranged from kitchen maids and laborers to bank executives and college professors.

Arthur R. Wyatt, the volunteer who came to give his services part-time, remained to become the full-time Executive Director (without salary). He is a retired bank official, who gives this explanation of why other employment agencies, Federal and private, have not the time or personnel to handle applications of older men and women with detailed concentration.

"With us," says Mr. Wyatt, "fitting the job-seekers to the available jobs takes a minimum of ten hours of work per placement. It starts with interviewing and listing qualifications which require nearly always an hour, and frequently much longer, when you include the necessary counseling. No applicant is ever hurried; the very fact that he is being interviewed by a person of his own age in itself proves reassuring." Dr. Theodore Halbert Wilson, President Emeritus of the University of Baltimore, became Chairman of the Board. Many other retired men and women, all community leaders, have been with the organization since its early days. Chairman Wilson calls this "a refreshing illustration of the ability and willingness of people, including the elderly, to meet needs of their fellow older citizens by creating and operating a private enterprise agency to which men and women can come for kindly counsel and friendly assistance."

His words are borne out by the fact that on an average day a staff of approximately forty volunteers interviews applicants and tries to place them in one or another of about three hundred listed job openings. A grant secured through the Maryland Commission on the Aging is recognition of the place the Service has won. The organization with its new funds was able to move into more commodious quarters and pay nominal salaries for office personnel (some of whom give voluntary service as well). Neither employer nor applicant pays a fee. The annual budget is now around $14,500, met chiefly by donations from individuals, industries, and local foundations.

Mr. Wyatt has some advice for any group of people who want to follow Baltimore's example. He believes one essential is "a dedicated staff to whom work is a habit and a pleasure in order to be able to secure three constant requirements: applicants, jobs and funds to carry on."

Mr. Wyatt's staff meets his own high qualifications. The supervisor of counselors is Mary S. Braun, a doctor of education from Johns Hopkins University, retired after years of teaching. Secretary of the organization is Mary T. McCurley. She is a former counselor in vocational guidance and a member of the Maryland Governor's Committee to Promote Employment of the Handicapped.

These are two typical placements:

1. A sixty-year-old woman interviewed in September, was not placed till May; then she became a bookkeeper in a large firm. She replaced a woman who had been forty-five years in the lawyers' employ, but she has successfully pleased the dozen lawyers in the firm.

2. A man with a good work record was interviewed in June and two weeks later was placed with a car rental firm. He has been promoted to office manager, and out of the gratitude he feels, he has offered the Over-60 Employment Counseling Service several job opportunities that have come his way.

If you would like to know how similar services can be set up in your own community, write

> Executive Director
> Over-60 Employment Counseling Service
> 300 N. Charles Street, Baltimore, Maryland 21201

CLEVELAND'S SENIOR COUNCIL

Although job-hunting is a perennial problem, there are many other outlets that have been developed in communities by retirees which did not exist before.

Although Cleveland's Senior Council as yet has no exact replica elsewhere, there is no reason why its plan of organization, relatively simple, should not be successful in any metropolis.

The Council, in existence since 1956, bears on its letterhead this clear statement of purposes and membership:

A tax-free gratis service organization of retired business executives and leaders in education and in the professions, qualified to act as counselors in a wide variety of projects in industry, transportation, banking, manufacturing, research, education, and welfare.

President Leslie P. Moyer, formerly an advertising executive, attributes much of the Council's success to its policy of supplying counsel and advice free of charge. "It not only maintains our tax-free status," he says, "in addition, it gives members a feeling that they are being of service to the community and doing something very worth while."

Unlike many organizations, the Council has never looked to Federal, state, or any kind of community support. The members pay annual dues (to do good!), and a number of important corporations in Cleveland have made contributions to the Council because they recognize its worth. It also is unlike other organizations of retired people in that it maintains a regularly staffed office with a paid executive at the head.

This outline of its organization and its methods provides suggestive reasons for its success, and the host of letters exchanged by the Council's officers with people in other communities indicate they would like to follow its example.

1. The Cleveland Senior Council was founded by retired community leaders concerned with creating opportunities for continued volunteer service by themselves and other retired men and women who had competence in one or more fields.

2. When it was organized in 1956 the purposes were outlined as follows:

> To supply helpful counsel on community projects which will enhance civic life and make it more attractive to its citizens;

> To provide an organization of retired executives and professional people to which companies and institutions may refer their retirees for membership and community activity;

> To provide counselling service from its reservoir of experts' talents for individuals and organizations;

> To provide means of educating companies so they will recognize the necessity of providing pre-retirement preparation for their personnel;

> To encourage activities with the aim of encouraging members to utilize their abilities to solve community problems.

All these aims have been accomplished. In its report of one year's activity, clients included the Regional Hospital Planning Board, Junior Achievement, a suburban Montessori school, the Muscular Dystrophy Society, a job training and placement shop, an eye clinic, and a host of individuals. All of them were given counsel by one or more than one of the hundred and sixty members who represent more than fifty areas of experience, nicknamed by a local wit, "Cleveland's Executive Reserve Force." Here is a sample of the advice given individuals:

Elderly engineer	Had design for heat exchanger device; suggestions given on patent protection and marketing
Elderly salesman	Advice on marketing a new type of teflon brushes
Manager, tuxedo rental shop	Counseling on financial problems, relocation, and pricing

Sales	Advice on marketing new place mat idea
Partners, attorney and engineer	Planning a new business; counseling on financing, customers, contacts
Woman (a secretary)	Advice on marketing a new type of teflon brushes
Elderly lapidarist	Counseling on advertising and marketing semi-precious stones and jewelry crafts

And so on through a long list; included in it are suggestions and advice given by telephone and many referrals to the proper organizations the inquirers did not know about, and should.

What the organization is *not* is as important as what it *is*. It is not an employment agency, although the Executive Director (an ex-newspaperwoman of long experience) and the Board have had many occasions to refer qualified people for posts they are fitted for. The Council is not a fund-raising organization for itself or for any other body, although many of its members are active in Cleveland campaigns on behalf of organizations they are interested in.

Monthly luncheon meetings promote fellowship among members; new ones can be nominated by anyone already in the Council who believes his nominee (a prospective retiree or someone already retired) has talents that can be put to work on behalf of others. Annual dues are $25, though some members make additional donations up to $100 a year. In effect, as the President points out, "Members pay from their own pockets for the opportunity to give their counsel away to those they can help."

If the Council seems to function somewhat like a club, it does, with this important exception. The individuals who comprise it are dedicated to just one idea; they believe that jointly they can either supply answers to problems presented to them or tell an inquirer where he is most likely to find his solution and help him make the contacts to get it. The nature of queries that come by the hundreds from anxious men and women indicate the place the organization has won for itself in the confidence of fellow citizens. Here is a sampling:

A retired schoolteacher wanted to find out how she could continue working with young people. A Council member, formerly a member of the Board of Education, counseled her, as he did the elementary school principal who wanted to get retired teachers to aid new members on his staff.

A foreman had questions about retirement. He was only forty-five years old, but he felt he ought to be planning for the years ahead but did not know how. A retirement plan was worked out with him.

Owner of a sheet metal company with a growing business needed accurate information on costs and how to get the right kind of new sales help. He had approached the Council five years before for advice and had acted on the suggestions his advisors had made and was well satisfied with their results.

Thus, Council members live up to their aim of "keeping in touch with the life-stream of Cleveland activities."

Because of the personal nature of its services, the Council never advises on problems by mail, or outside the greater Cleveland area. But it does answer letters of inquiry about its organizational plan. Individuals interested in finding out how to form a Council similar to its own, or who have questions relating to their own proposed organization, can write

The President
Cleveland Senior Council
1066 Hanna Building,
Cleveland, Ohio 44115

EXPERIENCE, INC., ST. LOUIS

The beginnings of this civic organization a considerable number of years ago is a valuable insight to what can happen in any community that has men and women of purpose living in it.

When William Charles was asked to become chairman of a committee of a hundred citizens to report to the community of St. Louis, Missouri, on whether or not an increase in the school tax rate was justified at that time, he had no previous connection with the Board of Education or those responsible for bringing the citizens' committee into existence. He learned that prior to coming to him they had approached, without success, several civic organizations in the community in an effort to find someone who would be willing to undertake the job of chairman.

It occurred to Mr. Charles then that there must be many other retired executives who had both the time and experience to do a civic job, but being in retirement meant they were apt often to be forgotten. Perhaps, he thought, something could be done to get them all into one organization. If that could be accomplished and the leaders in the city informed that such a group existed, then it could form a valuable pool of experienced people available when required to help solve almost any community problem. A number of retired executives and professional people with whom the idea was discussed thought well of it. The result was a series of luncheons to which additional retired executives were invited until there were finally sixteen interested in forming an organization along the lines Mr. Charles had originally outlined, and willing to work to bring it into existence. They had nothing but experience to contribute, so under the name of "Experience, Inc." they organized an nonprofit corporation under the laws of Missouri. In addition to taking part in other local matters, they decided to have as their chief purpose help to small business concerns in management problems.

This continued till the advent of SCORE, the federal organization that uses the same technique of asking retired executives to do business counseling. (See Chapter VII.) When the flow of local inquiries from business concerns diminished, the Board then decided to investigate the possibilities of sponsoring another special project to fill some local urgent need. The result was Opportunity, Inc., a plant set up to train handicapped men and women to execute subcontract work for business concerns in St. Louis. It still exists, is still sponsored by Experience, Inc., and still follows its original pattern.

Although St. Louis supports other organizations interested in rehabilitation of the disabled, Opportunity, Inc. has won for itself a place as a genuinely sound business enterprise. It was conceived, not for the profit of any owners, but for the benefit of the workers. (Somebody once called it "Communism, American style!") From the beginning its unpaid executives have been members of Experience, Inc., and its contract work from St. Louis businesses has also been obtained by them.

If you have ever had the idea that some enterprise in your hometown, with people like yourself behind it, could be advantageously run for the benefit of men and women who need work, the principles that the organizers of Opportunity, Inc. followed should offer some guidelines. (Obviously they would be applicable to enterprises other than those for the handicapped.)

1. Initial capital was small, amounting to some $6,500, raised among members and friends of members of Experience, Inc.

2. The first workers were only six disabled people. They successfully turned out work in a small building acquired by the Board. Firms from whom contracts were secured furnished all raw materials, and sometimes the machinery to execute the work. This was not "charity" but sound business practice. The six workers formed the nucleus for employing others as subcontracts were secured.

3. The plant has been managed by two members of Experience, Inc., one an electrical engineer, the other a former executive of a shoe company. The unpaid "salesmen" are other members of the parent organization.

4. The quality of work is indicated by the fact that securing subcontracts is not a problem now because there have been many repeat orders. The number of disabled workers in training, or working regularly on the job, averages forty. Some take other factory posts when they finish their training, and then others come in their stead.

5. Opportunity, Inc. has always operated "in the black." Its sponsor, Experience, Inc., determined it should be a sound business enterprise, not a charity. It has never asked for nor received a subsidy.

6. All prices are given on a strictly competitive basis. Opportunity, Inc. never offers to do by hand what can be done better by machine in a firm's own factory or by other subcontractors.

7. Employees have always received more than the U.S. minimum wage, plus proportionate shares of the modest profits, paid quarterly. In addition, a reserve fund has also gradually been built up out of profits, to insure continuation of the plant as long as it is needed.

In the words of the first President of Experience, Inc., William Charles, a retired accountant and civic leader, "Experience, Inc. has given the retired executive an opportunity to create a place for himself in the community and to repay at least in part what we all owe to the place in which we live."

If you are interested in the principles and procedures that are behind Opportunity's modest success as a self-supporting non-profit enterprise, write

President
Opportunity, Inc.
1711 Hereford St.
St. Louis, Missouri 63110

BOSTON'S CIVIC CENTER AND CLEARING HOUSE

Showing that it is possible to strike out in an entirely new direction, even in a community with centuries-old traditions, the Civic Center and Clearing House of Boston owes its existence primarily to a challenge given by John W. Putnam. At fifty, this self-styled "refugee from business" began with a few like-minded people, among them retirees, a new approach to the use of leisure time. It was one, they felt, that should be meaningful to the community, as well as the individual, and depart from usual philanthropic developments. The door should be open, its modest leaflet said, "to individuals of all ages seeking satisfying volunteer second careers and opportunities for participation in community service."

The largely volunteer staff (aided now by some small foundation grants) gives counsel to individuals who come to it and sometimes steers them to the usual paths of service in hospitals or other institutions. But the counselors not only have knowledge of Boston's organizations and agencies and their needs, they also know of some goals the usual philanthropies do not deal with at all. Furthermore, they have a different emphasis, expressed by the founder in these words: "Our first task, as we see it, is to find out what we can do for the individual who comes to us; our second concern is the institution or organization which he will serve."

Since Boston's Civic Center and Clearing House was started on a modest scale in 1961 it has achieved some widely acclaimed accomplishments (capable of application anywhere).

1. Volunteers interested in conservation undertook the first shade-tree survey in the history of Boston; it has been heralded as a distinct contribution to the resources program in this history-conscious city.

2. A project that developed out of the foregoing, involved the cataloguing of historic trees. One retiree, formerly with the John Hancock Insurance Company, uncovered an old elm on the Boston Common which enthusiasts believe is the same one planted under the direction of John Hancock himself, in 1780.

Not all projects stray so far from the beaten path of service. The Center arranged for volunteers on its rolls to staff a tourist center for the Department of Commerce and Development. They also plan to keep the International Section of Logan Airport staffed with volunteers possessing a knowledge of foreign languages.

Often the Clearing House's projects involve in preparatory educational program that is satisfying to participants. One such centered around collections of information about historic plaques and site markers.

What do volunteers think of this new approach to leisure-time activity? Here is what one retired teacher wrote:

The activity which I chose, work on the catalogue of Boston-owned art accessible to the public outside the museums, opened a new field of interest to me and still continues to enrich my knowledge of our city. The workers on this particular project are devoted in the time and effort they give to it.

Not everything has to be, or is aimed to be, on a high intellectual scale. Due chiefly to the persistence and hard work of two volunteers, the Boston *Globe* agreed to print a weekly column appealing for service by citizens on behalf of the city's major philanthropies. It was the Civic Center and Clearing House that lived up to its name by working on the plan in cooperation with Boston agencies, and it is the Center that supervises and coordinates answers to the continuous stream of letters received through publicity in the column about agencies' needs.

If you too have had ideas that may have seemed "revolutionary" to your contemporaries, and yet would like to see them developed in your community, talk them over with someone who has struck out in new directions. The Civic Center and Clearing House has a Board that feels Boston's ideas can be adapted to fit local conditions elsewhere. Write

Executive Director
Civic Center and Clearing House
14 Beacon St., Room 108, Boston, Massachusetts 02108

The Commonality of Brotherhood

Numerous retired people, diverse in character and background, are blazing many other new trails. Not everyone, however, has had the honor of providing the Federal Administration on Aging with a list of independent retirees who on their own initiative had formed organizations, modeled at last in part, on his own effort to see that people make use of their talents late in life.

This is only one of the many distinctions that Maurice du Pont Lee can claim. When he was seventy-seven—in 1962—he described himself "at the zenith of my second career," and well into his eighties showed no signs of losing interest in helping others lead a good life.

Mr. Lee is one of the wise people who had his post-retirement plans well in hand before he reached retirement age. He was then one of the executives of the du Pont Company in Wilmington, Delaware. He could have sat back and rested on his laurels, but he had long had a plan in mind which he immediately put into effect.

Because he had been called on many times to assist several small business owners to get on their feet, he determined to ask other retired executives to help him set up an organization that would give advice to people with business problems.

The result was the still loosely organized Consulting and Advisory Service made up of retired bankers, lawyers, accountants, engineers, and others who were recruited in this fashion:

1. With a few friends to advise him, Mr. Lee drew up a list of the retired and about to be retired men in Wilmington, of the caliber who could probably aid local businesses in trouble.

2. The next step was a meeting place; a bank was asked to donate its board room for the first and subsequent meetings. (Banks sent representatives because some small businesses, borrowing money, were their clients, and they realized the new counseling service would be in a position to detect business troubles before they grew too acute.)

3. Twenty of those invited came to the first meeting; fifty to the second; they formed the nucleus of the new organization of which leading business firms had been informed.

Consulting and Advisory Services has never charged or accepted a fee for anything done. It long ago branched out to include retired purchasing agents; corporation lawyers; architects, artists; experts in trade analysis, packing, accounting, real estate—and a wide variety of others. Practically every business problem has been met and conquered. Wide national publicity resulted in a still flowing mass of correspondence and requests to Mr. Lee to make speaking engagements. When he complies (and he often follows up his conferences with consultation with individuals) he insists that all he does is give "suggestions and advice based on what I accumulated in forty-five years of business experience."

One example suffices to show his methods can be practiced anywhere. A merchant in a Southern city wrote to ask advice. His business was failing; what should he do? Mr. Lee replied, saying he could not give any direct help since he had never been in the community. Nevertheless, he suggested that the troubled man find three or four experienced fellow citizens willing to sit down and talk over his business worries with him. Mr. Lee recommended that he approach members of the Chamber of Commerce, his church, or a community club interested in civic matters, such as the Rotary or Kiwanis. Furthermore, Mr. Lee advised Mr. X. to tell the full truth about his tangled affairs, to be sure to say that he did not want their money but needed expert counsel. Mr. Lee also urged him to let his business friends know that if they allowed his company to fail they would be depreciating the value of business property the town needed, and if they aided him to find a way to straighten out his affairs it would redound to the advantage of everybody.

The man, sensible enough to write Mr. Lee frankly, was sensible enough to follow to the letter the advice he had solicited. He succeeded in interesting three or four reliable businessmen, all members of his own church. He is now out of trouble and has a sound status in the community. "It seemed to me," says Mr. Lee, "that what I said to him was a very simple and easy remedy to his particular problem."

All Mr. Lee's solutions are, on the surface at least, simple. The greatest one of all was pointing out to men like himself that they did not have to resign from community life when they left their business or professional careers. Retirees all over the country and several foreign governments—as disparate as France and Saudi Arabia—have inquired about his methods. In his opinion the only requisite is a sincere and deep-rooted desire to help somebody, somewhere. All his life Mr. Lee has been a vigorous opponent of talent waste. When he was in his eighties people were still writing him for advice about new, untried projects they would like to start. If you too would like to have honest opinions on your own ideas for a better community life, write,

Consulting and Advisory Service
5421 Nemours Building
Wilmington, Delaware 19898

Work Yet to Be Done

It has been reported time and again that the most interesting and potentially the most productive mail received by state commissions on the aging is from individuals who wish to do what they can to help originate programs and services for the aging in their communities. The reason for this is that at least half the older population in the United States still have a critical struggle to meet basic problems of maintenance and health. But experts think there is a tremendous potential in people, especially older people, to help themselves and each other.

It does not take a large amount of creative ability, money, or a tremendous output of energy to launch any worthwhile project. Often a good place to begin is through your club or your church, but you can also do your bit through any organization, whether it is a fraternal lodge or a state agency on aging or a new anti-poverty agency. (See Appendix for lists.) The important factor is to get started, and not only for the sake of the other person; to do something more than to live longer than your fathers did means taking some action.

In a rural area of northern Michigan older men and women did not wait for some organization to tell them what needed doing. They banded together to see that surplus foods were delivered to isolated men and women who needed them. Nor do you always have to wait for somebody else. During her weekly trips as a volunteer at the Willowbrook State School on Staten Island, New York, Mrs. Marion Bennett noticed there was a huge backlog of mending that never seemed to get done. She talked it over at the Senior Citizens Center of which she is a member. The result was a mending project that became part of the program of activities. Now, with eleven other women, Mrs. Bennett mends huge laundry-bags full of garments three mornings a week; they are delivered and picked up by the State School.

Retirement in today's terms never existed before; today's over-sixty-five-year-olds were born at a time when the average man worked about seventy hours a week, and died around forty; today the reverse is true. Even if you are only fifty you have already lived through more cultural, industrial, social, and economic changes than any previous generation knew, and at a greater speed, with a good chance of joining the two million who have already seen their eighty-fifth birthday go by. But living long years and being inactive can be a great burden; few people need to be reminded of that. But many more need to translate into action before it is too late the words of the famous psychiatrist, Dr. William C. Menninger. He said, "People who stay young despite their years do so because of an active interest that provides satisfaction through participation."

The Federal Government's Concern with Aging

The March of Legislative Action

Today one out of every ten Americans has already reached or passed his sixty-fifth birthday; at the turn of the century only every twenty-fifth person was sixty-five or over. This dramatic increase has been marked by rapid strides in legislation, particularly on the federal level. The U.S. Government's interest reflects both concern for the well-being of the individual, and consciousness of the largely untapped resources that older citizens represent for our country.

The following brief summary represents some of the legislative highlights of the past decade.

In 1961, the first White House Conference on Aging chartered national goals. It was historic in that it was partially responsible for enactment of the Older Americans Act of 1965, creation of the U.S. Administration on Aging, and spurred adoption of Medicare and Medicaid. Approximately 80 percent of the Conference's recommendations have been carried out.

In 1962 President John F. Kennedy issued an Executive Order establishing the President's Council on Aging to disseminate information to public and private agencies functioning in fields related to problems of older people.

In 1963 President Kennedy proposed to Congress the first comprehensive program of federal action on behalf of older men and women. He called for "an imaginative and far-reaching effort . . . in both public and private sectors of our society."

In 1964, President Lyndon B. Johnson issued an Executive Order that forbade, for the first time, discrimination in employment on the basis of age by federal contractors and subcontractors in the private sector.

In 1965 Social Security Amendments made the Medicare program a reality. That legislation, and the Older Americans Act of 1965, mark the longest step forward since enactment of the original Social Security Act in 1935. The Act created the Administration on Aging in the U.S. Department of Health, Education, and Welfare; it made possible grants for research, demonstration projects, and training programs in states and in communities, large and small, to encourage them to strengthen existing programs and to create new ones to enrich the lives of their older citizens.

In 1966 legislation was passed which provided social security benefits for almost all men and women aged seventy-two or over who had not previously been eligible for them.

In 1967 the Social Security Act was amended to provide an average increase of 13 percent to all beneficiaries, raising 800,000 persons aged sixty-five and over above the poverty line.

In 1968 the first law against age discrimination in employment went into effect. Businesses involved in interstate commerce which hired twenty-five persons or more were forbidden to discriminate in hiring or discharging employees on the basis of age alone. The law also affects employment agencies and trade unions, forbidding discrimination in hiring or advertising policies.

In 1968, also, the House of Representatives and the Senate concurred in passing a joint resolution authorizing a second White House Conference on the Aging. It is scheduled for 1971, when there are expected to be about twenty-one million people over sixty-five in the United States, compared to seventeen million at the time of the first White House Conference on Aging in 1961.

The Administration on Aging

"Serve as clearinghouse for information related to problems of the aged and aging . . . prepare, publish, and disseminate education materials dealing with the welfare of older people . . . gather statistics in the field of aging which other Federal agencies are not collecting." (Older Americans Act of 1965.)

This explanation of the mandate given the Administration on Aging makes it the one best place for information on anything relating to the older man or woman in American society. Any one of its publications can be had, *free of charge,* as long as the supply lasts. They fall into three categories: (1) for older people, (2) for the general public, (3) for people working with and for older people. For a complete list, write for

> *Publications, AoA*
> U.S. Department of Health, Education, and Welfare
> Administration on Aging, Washington, D.C. 20201

Among the publications prepared especially for older men and women are the following:

You—the Law—and Retirement, AoA Publication No. 800

Consumer Guide for Older People, AoA Publication No. 801

The Fitness Challenge—in the Later Years, AoA Publication No. 802

Are You Planning on Living the Rest of Your Life? (A preretirement planning booklet, for self-guidance), AoA Publication No. 803

Employment and Volunteer Opportunities for Older People (A fact sheet reporting on federal programs that offer opportunities for older people in employment and volunteer service as of January, 1968.)

The Administration on Aging, operating within the Social and Rehabilitation Service of the U.S. Department of Health, Education, and Welfare, is headed by a Commissioner appointed by the President of the United States.

REGIONAL OFFICES

Specialists are located in each Regional Office to assist states and communities; as far as their limited personnel permits, offices will answer individual queries.

Region I

John Fitzgerald Kennedy Federal Building
Boston, Massachusetts 02203

Serving Connecticut, Maine, Massachusetts, New Hampshire, Rhode Island, Vermont

Region II

Room 3842, 26 Federal Plaza
New York, New York 10007

Serving Delaware, New Jersey, New York, and Pennsylvania

Region III

220 7th Street, N.E.
Charlottesville, Virginia 22901

Serving District of Columbia, Kentucky, Maryland, North Carolina, Virginia, West Virginia, Puerto Rico, Virgin Islands

Region IV

Room 404, 50 Seventh Street, N.E.
Atlanta, Georgia 30323

Serving Alabama, Florida, Georgia, Mississippi, South Carolina, Tennessee

Region V

Room 712, New P.O. Building
433 W. Van Buren St.
Chicago, Illinois 60607

Serving Illinois, Indiana, Michigan, Ohio, Wisconsin

Region VI

601 E. 12th Street
Kansas City, Missouri 64106

Serving Iowa, Kansas, Minnesota, Missouri, Nebraska, North Dakota, South Dakota

Region VII

1114 Commerce Street
Dallas, Texas 75202

Serving Arkansas, Louisiana, New Mexico, Oklahoma, Texas

Region VIII

Room 10444, Federal Office Building
19th and Stout Streets
Denver, Colorado 80202

Serving Colorado, Idaho, Montana, Utah, Wyoming

Region IX

406 Federal Office Building
50 Fulton Street
San Francisco, California 94102

Serving Alaska, Arizona, California, Hawaii, Nevada, Oregon, Washington

President's Council on Aging
Health, Education, and Welfare Building
Washington, D.C. 20201

The Council was established by Executive Order, May, 1962. Its purpose is to make a continuing review of governmental responsibilities in the field of aging and to make recommendations to the President; it is also authorized to seek coordination of Federal programs, promote exchange of information among governmental agencies, and disseminate information to public and private organizations interested in problems of aging.

The Older American, the Council's first annual report (1963), is a portrayal of the situation that the aging population of 18,000,000 persons over sixty-five were facing at that time. (Illustrated.)

A Time of Progress for Older Americans, a combined report of events in 1965, 1966, 1967. (Illustrated.) Administration on Aging Publication No. 137.

Both publications can be purchased, as long as supplies last, from the Superintendent of Documents, U.S. Printing Office, Washington, D.C. 20402 ($.50).

Senate Special Committee on Aging
(twenty members)
Chairman, Senator Harrison A. Williams

In 1961 the Senate Rules Committee approved a resolution establishing the Senate Special Committee on Aging, thus crystallizing the awareness of Congress that the Federal government has a responsibility to make the lives of the constantly growing number of older Americans both more meaningful and more comfortable. To this end the chief objective of the Committee has been to bring new opportunities of every kind to older men and women in all walks of life. It therefore makes a continuous study of all phases of problems that affect them, holds hearings on current questions, reports and publishes its findings, and makes recommendations for appropriate legislation, such as the Older Americans Act of 1965. The wide and watchful range of its activities is indicated by the nature of its subcommittees:

Subcommittee on Consumer Interests of the Elderly
Subcommittee on Employment and Retirement Income
Subcommittee on Federal, State, and Community Services
Subcommittee on Health of the Elderly

Subcommittee on Housing for the Elderly
Subcommittee on Long-term Care
Subcommittee on Retirement and the Individual

The published hearings are for sale by the U.S. Government Printing Office; for a list and prices, write the Superintendent of Documents, Washington, D.C. 20402. For information about the Committee's activities, write the Chief of Staff, Senate Special Committee on Aging, Senate Office Building, Washington, D.C. 20510.

Special Help for Older Workers

The Congress acknowledged the special needs of middle-aged and older Americans in an Amendment to the Manpower Development and Training Act of 1966, which stated:

The Secretary of Labor shall provide, where appropriate, a special program of testing, counseling, selection and referral of persons 45 years of age or older for occupational training and further schooling designed to meet the special problems faced by such persons in the labor market.

Charles E. Odell, Director of the U.S. Employment Service, states that the U.S. Employment Service and its affiliated State Employment Services expect to carry out this mandate by providing to each middle-aged and older person "the broadest possible freedom of choice on a continuum of employment and training opportunity which ranges from an immediate job in competitive employment to an opportunity for volunteer service."

The following cities have special Older Worker Service Units, with a staff trained to do counseling and placement and give advice to those over forty-five, though each State Employment Service has a staff able to aid workers of all ages.

Baltimore	Kansas City	Philadelphia
Boston	Long Beach	Pittsburgh
Buffalo	Los Angeles	Providence
Chicago	Milwaukee	Rochester
Cincinnati	Minneapolis-St. Paul	St. Louis
Cleveland	Oakland	San Diego
Dallas	New Orleans	San Francisco
Detroit	New York City	Van Nuys
Houston		Washington, D.C.

Score (Service Corps of Retired Executives)

The U.S. Small Business Administration initiated SCORE in 1964. There are now nearly two hundred chapters in as many cities. For information about them and the SBA's national roster of retirees who act as counselors for small businesses that need help, write or call the nearest regional or branch office, or the national office, 1441 L Street, N.W., Washington, D.C. 20416.

Northeastern Area

Augusta, Maine 04330
Federal Bldg., U. S. Post Office
40 Western Avenue

Boston, Massachusetts 02203
John Fitzgerald Kennedy Federal
Bldg.
Government Center

Concord, New Hampshire 03301
55 Pleasant Street

Hartford, Connecticut 06103
Federal Office Bldg., 450 Main
Street

Montpelier, Vermont 05601
Federal Bldg., P.O. and Courthouse
2nd Floor, 87 State Street

Providence, Rhode Island 02903
702 Smith Bldg., 57 Eddy Street

New York Area

Buffalo, New York 14203*
Federal Bldg., 121 Ellicott Street

Hato Rey, Puerto Rico 00919
255 Ponce De Leon Avenue
P.O. Box 1915

Newark, New Jersey 07102
970 Broad Street, Room 1636

New York, New York 10007
26 Federal Plaza 3108

Syracuse, New York 13202
Hunter Plaza, Fayette and Salina
Streets

Middle Atlantic Area

Baltimore, Maryland 21202
1113 Federal Bldg.
31 Hopkins Plaza, Charles Center

Charleston, West Virginia 25301*
3000 U.S. Courthouse and Federal
Bldg.
500 Quarrier Street, Room 3000

Cincinnati, Ohio 45202*
5026 Federal Building

Clarksburg, West Virginia 26301
Lowndes Bank Bldg.
119 N. 3rd Street

---

*indicates branch office

Cleveland, Ohio 44113
Standard Bldg., 1370 Ontario Street

Columbus, Ohio 43215
Beacon Bldg., 50 W. Gay Street

Dover, Delaware 19901
21 the Green

Louisville, Kentucky 40202
1900 Commonwealth Bldg.
Fourth and Broadway

Philadelphia, Pennsylvania 19107
Jefferson Bldg., 1317 Filbert Street

Pittsburgh, Pennsylvania 15222
Federal Bldg.
1000 Liberty Avenue

Richmond, Virginia 23226
P.O. Box 8565, 1904 Byrd Avenue

Toledo, Ohio 43602*
Federal Office Bldg.
234 Summit Street

Washington, D.C. 20417
1405 I Street, N.W.

Southeastern Area

Atlanta, Georgia 30309
1401 Peachtree Street, N.E.

Birmingham, Alabama 35205
S. 20th Bldg., 908 S. 20th Street

Charlotte, North Carolina 28202
Addison Bldg., Suite 500
222 South Church Street

Columbia, South Carolina 29201
1801 Assembly Street

Jackson, Mississippi 39205
P.O. Box 2351, U.S.P.O. and
Courthouse Bldg.

Jacksonville, Florida 32202
Federal Office Bldg.
400 W. Bay St., P.O. Box 35067

Knoxville, Tennessee 37902
Fidelity Bankers Bldg.
Room 307, 502 Gay Street

Miami, Florida 33130
912 Federal Office Bldg.
51 S.W. First Avenue

Nashville, Tennessee 37219
Security Federal Savings and Loan
Building
500 Union Street

Midwestern Area

Chicago, Illinois 60604
Federal Office Bldg., Room 437
219 South Dearborn Street

Des Moines, Iowa 50309
New Federal Building, Room 749
210 Walnut Street

Detroit, Michigan 48226
1200 Book Bldg., 1249 Washington
Blvd.

Indianapolis, Indiana 46204
36 South Pennsylvania Street

Kansas City, Missouri 64106
911 Walnut Street

Madison, Wisconsin 53703
25 West Main Street

Marquette, Michigan 49855
502 West Kaye Avenue

Milwaukee, Wisconsin 53203
Straus Building
238 W. Wisconsin Avenue

Minneapolis, Minnesota 55402
Reimann Bldg., 812 Second Ave. S.

St. Louis, Missouri 63102
Federal Building
208 N. Broadway

Southwestern Area

Albuquerque, New Mexico 87101
Federal Bldg. and U.S. Court House
Suite 3509
500 Gold Avenue, S.W.

Dallas, Texas 75201
Mayflower Bldg.
411 N. Akard Street

Harlingen, Texas 78550
219 East Jackson Street

Houston, Texas 77002
Niels Esperson Bldg.
808 Travis Street

Little Rock, Arkansas 72201
377 P.O. and Courthouse Bldg.
600 West Capitol Avenue

Lubbock, Texas 79401
204 Federal Office Bldg.
1616 19th Street

Marshall, Texas 75670
201 Travis Terrace Bldg.

P.O. Box 1349
505 East Travis Street

New Orleans, Louisiana 70130
124 Camp Street
P.O. Box 30564

Oklahoma City, Oklahoma 73102
Room 511, Oklahoma Mortgage
  Bldg.
324 North Robinson Ave.

San Antonio, Texas 78205
301 Broadway
300 Manion Building

Rocky Mountain Area

Casper, Wyoming 82601
Western Bldg.
300 North Center Street

Denver, Colorado 80202
Federal Office Bldg.
1961 Stout Street

Fargo, North Dakota 58102
300 American Life Bldg.
207 North Fifth Street

Helena, Montana 59601
P.O. Box 1690
205 Power Block
Corner, Main and 6th Avenue

Omaha, Nebraska 68102
7425 Federal Bldg.
215 North 17th Street

Salt Lake City, Utah 84111
2237 Federal Bldg.
125 South State Street

Sioux Falls, South Dakota 57102
502 Nat'l. Bank of S. Dakota Bldg.
8th and Main Avenue

Wichita, Kansas 67202
302 120 Bldg.
120 South Market Street

Pacific Coastal Area

Agana, Guam 96910*
Ada Plaza Center Bldg.
P.O. Box 927

Anchorage, Alaska 99501
632 Sixth Avenue, Suite 450

Boise, Idaho 83702
Room 408, Idaho Bldg.
216 North Eighth Street

Fairbanks, Alaska 99701*
510 Second Avenue

Honolulu, Hawaii 96913
1149 Bethel Street
Room 402

Las Vegas, Nevada 89101*
300 Las Vegas Blvd., S.
Room 4-104

Los Angeles, California 90014
849 South Broadway

Phoenix, Arizona 85004
Central Towers Bldg.
2727 N. Central Avenue

Portland, Oregon 97205
700 Pittock Block
921 S.W. Washington Street

San Diego, California 92101
110 West C Street

San Francisco, California 94102
Federal Bldg.
450 Golden Gate Avenue
Box 36044

Seattle, Washington 98104
1206 Smith Tower
506 Second Avenue

Spokane, Washington 99201
651 U.S. Court House
P.O. Box 2167

State Agencies Concerned with Older Americans

Most states have a special division, commission, or department whose chief concern is situations that confront older men and women. Others have designated existing departments to deal with such matters as retirement problems, housing, employment, and health. All of them can answer many questions regarding local matters.

Alabama Commission on Aging
459 S. Goldthwaite St., Montgomery 36104

Alaska Department of Health and Welfare
Pouch H. Juneau 99801

Arizona Division of Aging, Department of Public Welfare
1624 West Adams St., Phoenix 85007

Arkansas Office on Aging
State Capitol Building, Little Rock 72201

California Commission on Aging
1108 Fourteenth St., Sacramento 95814

Colorado Division of Services for the Aging
State Department of Social Services, 1600 Sherman St., Denver 80203

Connecticut Commission on Services for Elderly Persons
19 Washington Street, Hartford 06115

Delaware Commission for the Aging
P.O. Box 57, Dupont Parkway, N., Smyrna 19977

District of Columbia Interdepartmental Committee on Aging, Department of Public Welfare
122 C St., N.W., Room 803, Washington, D.C. 20001

Florida Commission on Aging
1309 Thomasville Road, Tallahassee 32303

Georgia State Commission on Aging
Room 224, 881 Peachtree St. N.E., Atlanta 30309

Guam Department of Public Health and Social Services
Box 2186, Agana 96910

Hawaii State Commission on Aging
1040 Ahiahi Street, Honolulu 96817

Idaho Office of the Governor
State Capitol, Boise 83702

Illinois Division of Community Services, Department of Public Aid
State Office Building, Springfield 62706

Indiana Commission on the Aging and Aged
1015 New State Office Bldg., Indianapolis 46204

Iowa Commission on Aging
State Office Bldg., East 14th and Grand, Des Moines 50319

Kansas Division of Services for the Aging, State Department of Social Welfare
State Office Building, Topeka 66612

Kentucky Commission on Aging
State Office Building, Frankfort 40601

Louisiana Commission on the Aging
P.O. Box 4482, Capitol Station, Baton Rouge 70804

Maine Services for the Aging, Department of Health and Welfare
State House, Augusta 04330

Maryland Commission on Aging
State Office Building, 301 W. Preston Street, Baltimore 21201

Massachusetts Commission on Aging
19 Milk Street, Boston 02109

Michigan Commission on Aging
1101 South Washington Ave., Lansing 48913

Minnesota Governor's Citizens Council on Aging
555 Wabasha, Room 204, St. Paul 55101

Mississippi Council on Aging
316 Wollfolk State Office Building, Jackson 39205

Missouri Office of Aging, Department of Community Affairs
501 Jefferson Building, Jefferson City 65101

Montana Commission on Aging
410 Mitchell Building, Helena 59601

Nebraska Advisory Committee on Aging
State House Station 94784, Lincoln 68509

Nevada Division of Welfare, Department of Health and Welfare
201 S. Fall Street, Carson City 89701

New Hampshire Committee for the Older Americans Act
One South Street, Concord 03301

New Jersey Division on Aging, Department of Community Affairs
P.O. Box 2768, Trenton 08626

New Mexico Older Americans Program, Community Development
Division
Health and Social Services Department, P.O. Box 2348, Santa Fe 87501
New York State Office for the Aging
11 N. Pearl Street, Albany 12207

North Carolina Governor's Coordinating Council on Aging
Administration Bldg., 116 W. Jones Street, Raleigh 27603

North Dakota Public Welfare Board
State Capitol Building, Bismarck 58501

Ohio Administration on Aging, Department of Mental Hygiene and Correction
State Office Building, Columbus 43215

Oklahoma Special Unit on Aging, Department of Public Welfare
Box 25352, Capitol Station, Oklahoma City 73125

Oregon Program on Aging
1479 Moss St., Eugene 97403

Pennsylvania Office of Family Services
Department of Public Welfare, Health and Welfare Building, Harrisburg 17120

Puerto Rico Gericulture Commission
Department of Health, P.O. Box 9342, Santurce 60908

Rhode Island State Division on Aging
25 Hayes Street, Providence 02908

Samoa (American) Lieutenant Governor
Pago Pago 96920

South Carolina Interagency Council on Aging
1001 Main Street, Room 218, Columbia 29601

South Dakota State Planning Agency
State Capitol Bldg., Pierre 57501

Tennessee Commission on Aging
510 Gay St., Capitol Towers, Nashville 37219

Texas Governor's Committee on Aging
Box 12125, Capitol Station, Austin 78711

Utah Council on Aging, Department of Health and Welfare
116 State Capitol Bldg., Salt Lake City 84114

Vermont Interdepartmental Council on Aging
118 State Street, Montpelier 05602

Virginia Commission on the Aging
9th Street Office Bldg., 9th and Grace Streets, Richmond 23219

Virgin Islands Commission on Aging
Charlotte Amalie, P.O. Box 539, St. Thomas 00801

Washington State Council on Aging
P.O. Box 1162, Olympia 98501

West Virginia Commission on Aging
Room 410, Professional Bldg., 1036 Quarrier St., Charleston 25301

Wisconsin Division on Aging, Department of Health and Social Services
State Office Bldg., Room 690, 1 West Wilson St., Madison 53702

An annual meeting of the National Conference of State Executives, sponsored by the U.S. Administration on Aging, is held in Washington in conjunction with a Conference of the National Association of State Units on Aging. At the meetings held in October, 1968, an attempt was made to outline possible developments in the lives of older people as far ahead as the twenty-first century.

Information in Rural Areas

A principal source is the Specialist in Human Relations, Human Development, or Family Life and Parent Education on a state level. For information that cannot be obtained locally, write or call them, or the Human Development and Human Relations Specialist, Federal Extension Service, U.S. Department of Agriculture, Washington, D.C. 20250. (An asterisk (*) indicates states without specialists; title of contact person is listed.)

State	Title	Headquarters
Alabama	Specialist in Human Development	Auburn University Auburn 36830
*Alaska	State Home Economics Leader or Home Demonstration Agent	Box B, University of Alaska, College 99735; or Box 400, Nome 99762
Arizona	Extension Specialist in Human Relations and Child Development	Home Economics Building University of Arizona Tucson 85721
Arkansas	Extension Human Relations Specialist	Post Office Box 391 Little Rock 72203
California	Extension Specialist in Family Relations and Leadership Training	275 University Hall 2200 University Avenue University of California Berkeley 94720

State	Title	Headquarters
Colorado	Home Economics Program Leader or Family Relations Consultant	Colorado State University Fort Collins 80521
Connecticut	Human Relations Specialist	University of Connecticut Storrs 06268
*Delaware	State Leader, Home Economics Extension	University of Delaware Newark 19711
Florida	Family Life Specialist	Florida State University Tallahassee 32306
Georgia	Extension Home Economist-Family Life Specialist	University of Georgia Athens 30601
*Hawaii	Leader of Family Living	2525 Varney Circle University of Hawaii Honolulu 96822
*Idaho	State Home Economics Leader	Box 300 Boise 83701
Illinois	Extension Specialist in Family Life	College of Agriculture University of Illinois Urbana 61801
Indiana	Extension Specialist, Child-Adult Development and Family Relationships	Purdue University Lafayette 47907
Iowa	Extension Specialist, Human Development and Family Life; Extension Assistant in Child Development	Iowa State University Ames 50010
Kansas	Extension Family Life Specialist	Kansas State University Manhattan 66504
Kentucky	Extension Specialist in Family Life	121 Washington Avenue University of Kentucky Lexington 40506

State	Title	Headquarters
Louisiana	Associate Specialist in Family Life-Aging	Louisiana State University Baton Rouge 70803
Maine	Extension Specialist in Family Life	University of Maine Orono 04473
Maryland	Extension Family Life Specialist	University of Maryland College Park 20742
Massachu- setts	Extension Human Devel- opment (Professor)	Hampshire House University of Massachusetts Amherst 01003
Michigan	Extension Specialist in Family Life	103 Home Economics Bldg. Michigan State University East Lansing 48823
Minnesota	Extension Specialist in Family Life	University of Minnesota St. Paul 55101
Mississippi	Extension Family Life Specialist	Mississippi State University State College 39762
Missouri	Human Development and Family Life Specialist; or Child Development Special- ist	35 Stanley Hall University of Missouri Columbia 65201
Montana	Extension Specialist in Human Development	Montana State University Bozeman 59715
*Nebraska	Assistant Director	109 Agricultural Hall College of Agriculture Lincoln 68503
Nevada	Family Life Specialist	School of Home Economics University of Nevada Reno 89507

State	Title	Headquarters
New Hampshire	Extension Home Economist, Human Relations	University of New Hampshire, Durham 03824
New Jersey	Extension Specialist in Human Relations	Extension Service College of Agriculture New Brunswick 08903
*New Mexico	State Supervisor	New Mexico State University, Las Cruces 88001
New York	Extension Leader, Department of Child Development and Family Relationships	New York State College of Home Economics Cornell University Ithaca 14850
North Carolina	Family Relations Specialist or Area Extension Specialist in Aging	Post Office Box 5097 North Carolina State University, State College Station, Raleigh 27607
*North Dakota	Assistant Director for Family Living	North Dakota State University, Fargo 58103
Ohio	Extension Specialist, Home Management and Family Development	1787 Neil Avenue Ohio State University Columbus 43210
Oklahoma	Family Life Specialist	Cooperative Extension Service, State University Stillwater 74075
Oregon	Family Life Specialist or Home and Family Education Coordinator	161 Home Economics Oregon State University Corvallis 97331
Pennsylvania	Child Development and Family Life Specialist	Human Development South Pennsylvania State University, University Park 16802

State	Title	Headquarters
Puerto Rico	Family Life Specialist	Extension Service, Box 607 Rio Piedras 00927
*Rhode Island	State Home Demonstration Leader	University of Rhode Island Kingston 02281
South Carolina	Extension Family Life Specialist	Clemson University Clemson 29631
South Dakota	Extension Family Life Specialist	South Dakota State University Brookings 57007
*Tennessee	State Leader, Home Economics	College of Agriculture Knoxville 37901
Texas	Specialist in Family Life Education	Texas A & M University College Station 77841
*Utah	Extension Home Economics Program Leader	Utah State University Logan 84321
*Vermont	Supervisor and Program Leader	College of Agriculture Burlington 05401
Virginia	Extension Specialist in Family Life Education	Virginia Polytechnic Institute, Blacksburg 24061
*Virgin Islands	Home Economics Supervisor	Agricultural Experiment Station, Box 167 Kingshill Road St. Croix 00850
*Washington	State Leader, Home Economics Extension	Wilson Hall, 106 Washington State University, Pullman 99163
West Virginia	State Extension Child Development and Human Relations Specialist	107 Oglebay Hall West Virginia University Morgantown 26506

State	Title	Headquarters
Wisconsin	Extension Specialist, Child Development and Family Relations	148 Home Economics Bldg. University of Wisconsin Madison 53706
*Wyoming	State Extension Leader, Home Economics	University of Wyoming University Station Box 3354 Laramie 82071

Appendix C

National Council on the Aging

The Council is a nonprofit national organization that has for its focus the whole spectrum of questions that concern the older American. It was chartered in 1960 primarily to give assistance to community leaders, professional and civic groups, and government agencies. Its specialists help communities carry out projects, supervise demonstration programs, offer counsel, prepare special studies, and answer queries of individuals as well as agencies. The extensive library service includes preparation of bibliographies, research facilities, and loans of material. The Council is frequently represented at Congressional hearings concerned with problems of older men and women.

Membership is open to individuals as well as organizations. It includes reduced registration fees for regional and national conferences, priority in field service, and subscriptions to the NCOA *Journal,* the *Public Policy Bulletin, Centers Newsletter,* and the library's *Current Literature on Aging.*

> National Council on the Aging
> 315 Park Avenue, South
> New York, N.Y. 10010

Special Educational Opportunities

An increasing number of colleges and universities are taking note of the many older adults who would like to begin, continue, or recommence study, with or without a diploma in view. Certain others are taking cognizance of the fact that many men and women would like to know something about preparing for their retirement years.

Anyone interested should inquire at institutions of higher learning in his own area; if no such courses exist, enough requests by interested people may be a sufficient impetus to start them on what the Adult Education Association calls "the concept of lifelong learning."

The following are merely representative examples of the type of diverse opportunities open in various parts of the country.

Pre-Retirement Courses

The University of Michigan was the first in the country to schedule pre-retirement courses open to others besides regular students. It has made the basic reading material, in the form of brief pamphlets, available to the general public. They cover the fields of financial planning, physical and mental health, legal affairs, family and living arrangements, use of leisure, and so on. The booklet used in the last of the eleven-session course is

A Retirement Readiness Checklist
Prepared by Woodrow W. Hunter.
(Each booklet's price is $.30)

For a complete list of titles, plus other suggested reading and available films, write

Division of Gerontology, University of Michigan
1510 Rackham Building, Ann Arbor, Michigan

LOOKING AHEAD: PRE-RETIREMENT PLANNING

This is the title of a pre-retirement discussion series designed for people in their fifties who volunteered to attend workshops. The series was developed by the Adult Education Council of Metropolitan Denver, Colorado, and funded by governmental and state grants. Several Colorado colleges and universities have instituted similar training institutes, based on the Denver pattern. The syllabus prepared for the series by Dr. Lennig Sweet is available for general distribution. Write

Adult Education Council of Metropolitan Denver
1314 Acoma Street, Denver, Colorado 80204
Price $3.00, postage paid

RETIREMENT OPPORTUNITY PLANNING CENTER

This is the first experimental center in the nation designed to test and compare several different types of pre-retirement counseling. It opened at Drake University, Des Moines, Iowa, in September, 1967. With a grant from the Administration on Aging, the U.S. Department of Labor, and support from the Iowa Commission on Aging, and the University itself, five hundred participants annually in the Des Moines area (three hundred from industry and two hundred from the public-at-large) will participate in various kinds of discussions. The age range of enrollees is from fifty-seven to sixty-two, and they represent five target groups: industrial workers; white collar employees of large agencies; state government employees; members of professional and occupational associations; and individuals from the community at large. Spouses are included in counseling and activities.

The Administration on Aging's "Fact Sheet" says, "Particular emphasis will be given to development of interests for pre-retirees outside their present work situations in order to prepare them for productive activity and meaningful use of leisure time after full-time regular employment is past."

Program material, mimeographed or printed, is prepared for the courses. After testing with several control groups it may be made available to the public. For information, write

> Pre-Retirement Planning Center
> 2500 University Ave.
> Drake University, Des Moines, Iowa 50311

Lifetime Learning

Under this or similar names, a spate of diverse plans for offering retired men and women a chance to continue interrupted education, or who find they have fewer interesting activities than they would like, has sprung up all over the United States. Some of the more dramatic of the new educational ideas include the following:

Senior Citizens Program, the University of Kentucky. First of its kind in the nation, the Herman L. Donovan Senior Citizens Fellowship Program (named for the late President of the University of Kentucky) offers free tuition to anyone sixty-five or older, regardless of place of residence. Anyone is eligible to apply, including those with no high school diploma. Regular courses are included in the program, and all fees are waived. The plan was inaugurated in 1964 and produced its first graduate in 1967.

Under the Senior Citizens Program, the student may enroll in a curriculum leading to a degree, or attend classes in his or her special field of interest. Students with either aim use the program to further an interest in world affairs, bring professional techniques up to date, or to gather knowledge to resume a career or start a new one.

For more information or an application blank, write

> Council on Aging, University of Kentucky
> Lexington, Kentucky

A number of other colleges or universities have taken note of the fact there is no fixed timetable for learning. Several offer courses to adults past a certain age, without charge, on an extension program basis. The following represent some of the variations. Queries regarding similar plans should be addressed to institutions of higher learning in one's own state.

University Extension Class Program, Massachusetts State Department of Education. Enrollment is free to persons sixty-five and over. A wide variety of technical and craft courses is offered. For brochures, write

Massachusetts Commission on Aging
19 Milk Street, Boston, Massachusetts 02109

Home Study Programs. Programs in the liberal arts leading, if desired, to a diploma, are given for adults who live away from any college campus. Two of them to which queries may be addressed are

Syracuse University, Syracuse, New York
University of Oklahoma, Norman, Oklahoma

Institute of Retired Professionals. This adult educational venture is limited to five hundred individuals who are retired or semi-retired from professional or executive careers that have lasted at least twenty years. Its over-forty learning groups, ranging from philosophy to the theater, are led by member volunteers. They may also take one daytime course each semester with regular students at the New School for Social Research. Founded in 1962, its pattern has been adapted to other cities' educational programs for adults. For information, write

Director, Institute for Retired Professionals
New School for Social Research
66 West 12th Street, New York, N.Y. 10011

The Institute of Lifetime Learning. The pilot program, designed to overcome some barriers experienced by mature adults in other educational programs, was sponsored in the Washington, D.C. area by the American Association of Retired Persons and the National Retired Teachers Association for their members. Instruction is given at a college level by professors from nearby institutions of higher learning. Participants have a choice of more than sixty subjects, from art to lip-reading. The name is protected by copyright; certificates are issued, however, for similar programs in other communities sponsored by chapters of the national organizations. For information and location of the Institutes, write

American Association of Retired Persons (or)
National Retired Teachers Association

Eastern Headquarters:
1225 Connecticut Ave., N.W.
Washington, D.C. 20036

Western Headquarters:
Times Building, Long Beach, California 90802

The Oliver Wendell Holmes Association. This nonprofit educational organization is chartered by the Board of Regents of the University of the State of New York. Its aim is to bring together the "as yet largely untapped human resources of those who have reached retirement age" with "the invaluable human resources of emeriti professors who possess a sustained intellectual vigor and teaching skills." It accomplishes these aims by organizing institutes in broad fields of study, and a number have been held each year since 1963 in various parts of the United States. Each community must provide meeting facilities, transportation, maintenance, and fees for the faculty, for a period that varies from two to six weeks of lectures and seminars. For information, write

Oliver Wendell Holmes Association
381 Park Avenue, South
New York City, N.Y. 10016

Appendix E

Anti-poverty Programs

For information about any local or state anti-poverty program under the Office of Economic Opportunity, get in touch with the nearest regional office, or write

National Office
Office of Economic Opportunity
1200 Nineteenth Street, N.W.
Washington, D.C. 20506

Regional Offices, OEO

Northeast Region
72 W. 45th Street
New York, N.Y. 10036
Tel.: (212) 573-6361

States Included in Region
Connecticut, Maine, Massachusetts, New Hampshire, New Jersey, New York, Rhode Island, Vermont

Mid-Atlantic Region
1832 M Street, N.W.
Washington, D.C. 20036
Tel.: (202) 382-6383

Delaware, District of Columbia, Kentucky, Maryland, North Carolina, Pennsylvania, Virginia, West Virginia

	States Included in Region
Southeast Region 730 Peachtree St., N.E. Atlanta, Georgia 30308 Tel.: (404) 526-3337	Alabama, Florida, Georgia, Mississippi, South Carolina, Tennessee
Great Lakes Region 623 South Wabash Avenue Chicago, Illinois 60605 Tel.: (312) 353-5786	Illinois, Indiana, Michigan, Minnesota, Ohio, Wisconsin
Southwest Region Lowich Building 314 West 11th Street Austin, Texas 78701 Tel.: (512) 475-5717 Extension 6381	Arkansas, Louisiana, New Mexico, Oklahoma, Texas
North Central Region 911 Walnut Street Kansas City, Missouri 64104 Tel.: (816) 374-2206	Colorado, Idaho, Iowa, Kansas, Missouri, Montana, Nebraska, North Dakota, South Dakota, Utah, Wyoming
Western Region 100 McAllister Street San Francisco, California 94102 Tel.: (415) 556-7716	Alaska, Arizona, California, Hawaii, Nevada, Oregon, Washington
Special Projects Office Community Action Program Office of Economic Opportunity Washington, D.C. 20506 Tel.: (202) 382-5165	Indian Reservations, Migrant Projects, Puerto Rico, Virgin Islands, Guam, Trust Territories of the Pacific

Appendix F

Publications

Booklets, Pamphlets, Leaflets, Newsletters
Free or Available at Small Cost

Banks, insurance companies, state commissions or committees on aging, departments of physical or mental health, and a number of organizations interested in the questions affecting older people, issue publications. Many contain current information on happenings of interest, or progress made on problems of the aging. The following are representative—note that many are free.

Added Years. Monthly. *Free.* Send name and address to

> Division on Aging
> P.O. Box 2768
> Trenton, New Jersey 06825

Adding Life to Years. Monthly. $1.00 a year. Contains four-page insert, usually prepared by some expert in an aspect of a current question. Address

> Institute of Gerontology
> University of Iowa
> 26 Byington Road
> Iowa City, Iowa 52240

Enriching the Added Years. U.S. Department of Health, Education, and Welfare, 1963. $.10. (If supply is exhausted, a new, revised edition sometimes takes its place, occasionally under a different name.) Ask for a complete list of publications dealing with aging:

Superintendent of Documents
U.S. Government Printing Office
Washington, D.C. 20402

A Full Life After Sixty-five, by Edith Stern, 1967. $.25

Public Affairs Pamphlets
381 Park Avenue, South
New York, N.Y. 10016

How to Retire and Like It, by Raymond P. Kaighn, 1965. Reissued in paperback, in condensed form, 126 pages. $.75

Association Press
291 Broadway
New York, N.Y. 10007

More Life for Your Years. Monthly fact sheet. *Free.* Send name and address to

American Medical Association
Committee on Aging
535 N. Dearborn Street
Chicago, Illinois 60601

Planning for the Later Years, April, 1968, 50 pages. $.35. Prepared by the Social Security Administration. Order from

Superintendent of Documents
U.S. Government Printing Office
Washington, D.C. 20402

Pre-Retirement Planning Program. Mimeographed. *Free.* A suggested program, containing query sheets to be filled out by the individual, not only about financial status, assets, and probable obligations, but blanks to be filled in by the reader, listing (a) current activities from dawn to dawn (b) activities you would *like* to be engaged in during same period of time during retirement. This self-analysis can be obtained from

> New Jersey Division on Aging
> P.O. Box 2768
> Trenton, N.J. 08625

Time of Progress for Older Americans, 1965-1966-1967, 58 pages. $.50. President's Council on Aging. Write

> Superintendent of Documents
> U.S. Government Printing Office
> Washington, D.C. 20402

Magazines

There are numerous books that deal with preparation for retirement, where and how to live, health, new careers, reemployment, financial affairs, and in fact practically any topic that may have crossed the mind of a person as he nears or passes his fiftieth birthday. Any library, large or small, will have at least some on its bookshelves, and the new ones are reviewed in the usual media, as well as in special magazines, like the following:

Aging, monthly, $2.00 a year, $.20 a copy. This is the newsletter of the Administration on Aging, intended both for individuals and for organizations, and for the layman as much as for the professional. It covers the federal and state field of activity, but also reports on local community programs. Each issue contains much of interest to older people, wherever located and whatever their status. Illustrated. Subscribe through

> Superintendent of Documents
> U.S. Government Printing Office
> Washington, D.C. 20402

Dynamic Maturity, Modern Maturity, and *NRTA Journal.* Each is a bimonthly, $2.00 a year, but only the first will accept subscriptions. The others are sent to members of one or the other parent organization:

> American Association of Retired Persons (or)
> National Retired Teachers Association
> 215 Long Beach Blvd., Long Beach, California 90802

Harvest Years, monthly, $4.50 a year, $.50 a copy. Successful ventures and current happenings of interest to people nearing retirement or already retired.

Harvest Years Publishing Co.
104 E. 40th Street
New York, N.Y. 10016

Retirement Almanac, annual, paperbound, $1.95, approximately 160 pages in 1968 edition. Discusses such topics as financial planning, health and medical matters, housing, longevity, travel.

Retirement Publications
Box 36, Cos Cob, Connecticut 08607

Professional Journals

While these journals are intended for serious practioners in the fields of geriatrics or gerontology, frequently they carry articles of interest and of moment to laymen. The journals can usually be found in any large public library.

Geriatrics. Monthly. Lancet Publications, Inc., 4015 W. 65th Street, Minneapolis, Minnesota 55435. $21.00 a year; $2.00 a copy.

Geriatric Times. A tabloid-sized monthly designed to cover news and developments in "gericare." Edwill Publications, Inc., 801 Second Avenue, New York, N.Y. 10017. $10.00 a year; $1.00 a copy.

The Gerontologist. Quarterly. Gerontological Society, 600 S. Euclid Ave., St. Louis, Missouri 63110. $10.00 per year; $2.50 per issue. Covers biological sciences, clinical medicine, psychological and social sciences, and social welfare.

Journal of Gerontology. Published by the same Society. Quarterly. $15.00 per year; $3.75 an issue. Carries articles of general interest, such as medical care, recreation, housing, social welfare, employment.

Journal of the American Geriatrics Society. Monthly. The William & Wilkins Co., 428 E. Preston Street, Baltimore, Maryland 21202. $10.00 a year; $1.50 a copy.

Journal of the American Society for Geriatric Dentistry. Quarterly. 431 Oakdale Avenue, Chicago, Illinois 60657.

Medical World News. Weekly. Medical World Publishing Co., Inc., 777 Third Avenue, New York, N.Y. 10017. $17.50 a year; $.75 a copy.

Index